OPPORTUNITIES

in

Forensic Science Careers

OPPORTUNITIES

in

Forensic Science Careers

REVISED EDITION

BLYTHE CAMENSON

New York Chicago San Francisco Lisbon London Madrid Mexico City
Milan New Delhi San Juan Seoul Singapore Sydney Toronto

Library of Congress Cataloging-in-Publication Data

Camenson, Blythe.
    Opportunities in forensic science careers / by Blythe Camenson.—2nd ed.
        p.   cm.
    Includes bibliographical references.
    ISBN 0-07-154533-6 (alk. paper)
      1. Forensic sciences—Vocational guidance.   2. Criminal investigation—
Vocational guidance.   I. Title.

   HV8073.C316   2008
   363.25023'73—dc22   2008022945

1 2 3 4 5 6 7 8 9 10 11 12 13 14 15 16 17 18 19 20   DOC/DOC   0 9 8

ISBN 978-0-07-154533-4
MHID   0-07-154533-6

Interior design by Rattray Design

This book is printed on acid-free paper.

CONTENTS

Forensic architecture. Wildlife forensics. Sample jobs.
A final thought.

Foreword

In addition to the expected areas of jobs in the service sector, professions in science and technology are expected to grow exponentially in the decades ahead. Projected job growth varies among occupational specialties, but forensic science professionals and technicians are expected to grow much faster than average. This is not unexpected as one considers the historical fascination with all things forensic. One might ponder why our prehistoric ancestors placed those fingerprints on early paintings and rock carvings. Was it just because they thought the pattern of the fingerprint was interesting? Or did they perceive the uniqueness of the fingerprint even then and leave undeniable proof of the artist's identity?

As early as the 700s A.D. Chinese used fingerprints to establish identity on important documents, and in the first millennium the Roman Quintilian introduced bloody palm prints as evidence that a blind man was framed for the murder of his mother (Rudin and Inman, 2002). Human beings distinguish themselves by their inquisitive nature and their need to ask questions, seek justice, and right wrongs. Forensic scientists are the champions of this quest.

Forensic science is the application of science to law; it involves precise and rigorous methods for the identification and presentation of empirical evidence to establish whether a crime has been committed and, if so, how and sometimes even why. Forensic science doesn't just involve identifying traces of evidence; sometimes it isn't obvious just what the evidence really is. Other questions that need to be addressed are how the evidence came to be at the crime scene, where it originally came from, and who left it there. Forensic science is based on the assumption that after any act of violence, crime, or traumatic event, evidence is always left behind—there is always some change in the environment; forensic science is concerned with the empirical identification and verification of the proof of that change.

Forensic science is the gatekeeper for justice; through forensic science, objective arguments are made establishing the validity of testimony and ultimately the convictions of those perpetrating crimes. Forensic science is the foundation upon which forensic careers are based, and this text introduces those careers, opening the doors to a veritable galaxy of career options. For, as science continues to expand our understanding of forensic phenomena and the knowledge by which we can investigate this evidence expands, we proliferate specialties in forensic science and our options are virtually limitless.

Contemporary realities have increased the public demand for resolution of crime; since 9/11, the American psyche has been transformed in ways that heighten our awareness of risk and our expectation that, through science, only effort and resources stand between an act of criminality and justice. Media and entertainment have increased our awareness of forensic science, and through TV shows such as "CSI," cultural awareness and interest in forensic science has grown; along with that so has an increase in forensic educational programs and careers. Forensic careers provide opportunities for almost any disposition or inclination; there is something for everyone. Forensic professionals work in settings as diverse as crime scene evidence recovery to the laboratory. Whether focusing on physical evidence at the microscopic level to the detection of chemicals to the documentation of physical debris at sites as large as an aircraft crash scene, forensic science has a role. Forensic applications in the behavioral sciences range from detached clinical observation of the behavior of suspected criminals to the in-depth analysis of human motivation and thought related to crime. Forensic careers include aspects of civil litigation; the investigation of forgeries, fraud, and negligence in the marketing of foods and drinks; the manufacture of products, foods, and chemicals; and the regulation of automobile emissions.

The broad body of knowledge necessary for forensic scientists and professionals to practice within the subspecialties of criminal/legal investigations or practice is incorporated in educational and professional programs ranging from certification courses and continuing education to academic and professional degrees. Forensic professional and academic specialties include criminalistics, engineering sciences, medical illustration, jurisprudence, odontology, pathology and biology, psychiatry and behavioral sciences, forensic medicine, document examination, toxicology, and entomology.

The field of behavior science is an expanding forensic specialty focusing on the analysis of human thinking and its relationship to deviant and criminal behavior. Such applications as profiling, psychological autopsy, detection of potential for violence, and assessment of competency are examples of forensic psychiatric practice. An entire science of *victimology*, or study of the characteristics and predictors of victims of crime, has emerged as a field within this specialty.

Computer investigations, examination of pollens and botanical evidence, along with anthropological evidence recovery of skeletal and artifacts remains represent expanding forensic science opportunities. One of the newest forensic professions, *forensic nursing*, is an example of what at first appears to be a poor fit—a health care profession and criminal investigation. But, like so many other marriages between a scientific-based profession and the law, forensic nursing is emerging as a specialty built on the clinical skills, competencies, and knowledge of human responses to illness and health alterations. Forensic nurses are adapting their roles to create a unique response to clinical investigation and treatment of interpersonal violence, injury, and exploitation, particularly among the vulnerable populations.

The appeal of forensic science and forensic professions to diverse groups of individuals is supported by the widely different applications. Developed from so many disciplines, forensic science appeals to equally diverse persons. In every forensic specialty, the principles of a specific discipline are applied to the analysis of physical evidence or human behavior to resolve legal issues. Most forensic professions require a minimum of a bachelor's degree in an applied field such as forensic science, chemistry, biology, physics, physical anthropology, or nursing. Individuals do not need to specialize at the undergraduate level, however, as a broad scientific background provides more flexibility when seeking a position.

Whether one is a chemist or botanist, physician or computer scientist, anthropologist or historian, perhaps the most important factor impacting success in a forensic profession is personality. The most valuable attributes of forensic scientists are summarized as: the ability to persevere when confronted with difficult tasks; insatiable curiosity and the desire to know the "how and why" as much as the "what"; the ability to think critically and patiently, focusing on detail; and comfort working both independently and as a team member. Exploring the possibility of a career as a forensic scientist affords the opportunity to work in an exciting, challenging, and valued profession dedicated to preserving justice through the pursuit of objective knowledge. Comparing and contrasting the essential characteristics, purpose, and requirements of different forensic specialties is prerequisite to choosing such a career.

Anita G. Hufft, Ph.D., R.N.
Dean and Professor
College of Nursing
Valdosta State University
Valdosta, Georgia

Acknowledgments

The author would like to thank the following professionals for providing information and advice on careers in the forensic sciences:

A. Midori Albert, forensic anthropologist
Jan Bailey, psychiatric technician
William Foote, forensic psychologist
Robert Lemons, fire investigator
Jack Murray, accident investigator
Sandra Ramsey Lines, forensic document examiner
George Reis, forensic digital imaging consultant
Randy Skelton, forensic anthropologist
Patricia Speck, forensic nurse
Douglas Ubelaker, forensic anthropologist

1

FORENSIC SCIENCE FIELDS

OVER THE YEARS, we've become nearly addicted to stories that deal with forensics. Television shows such as "CSI," "Law and Order," "Bones," "Forensic Files," "NCIS," "Cold Case," and "Without a Trace" are just some of the many programs that tell their stories through the use of forensic science. The forensic detectives created by authors such as Patricia Cornwell, James Patterson, and Jeffrey Deaver seem like old friends to regular readers. And all of this fiction is based on reality, as we read news reports about DNA evidence clearing people wrongly imprisoned for crimes they did not commit or helping to close old, unsolved cases.

In their study of crime scenes, forensic specialists assist police and attorneys by collecting and examining evidence such as fingerprints, hairs, fabric fibers, footprints, and so on. The hope is that this examination will lead to an arrest and trial, where a jury can decide between guilt and innocence. It's in the court of law where the term *forensic* is most often applied.

The word *forensic* is derived from the Latin word *forensis*, which means "of the forum." The forum is where the law courts of ancient Rome were held, so it makes sense that today's definition of *forensic* refers to the application of scientific principles and practices to the legal process, during which expert testimony often plays a role. In other words, the adjective *forensic* means pertaining to, connected with, or used in courts of law.

Forensic science is the acquisition and analysis of scientific data for application to the study and resolution of crime, investigation, civil and regulatory issues, and criminal identification.

Role of Forensic Sciences

The forensic sciences play an increasingly important role in our justice system, impacting far more than law enforcement alone. Forensic scientists may be involved in all aspects of a criminal case, and the results of their work may help either the prosecution or the defense. The point of forensic science is to use all the scientific information available to determine facts.

Forensic science can also help to resolve civil cases, since questions of law and fact may also require forensic science expertise. For example, a forensic scientist can attest to the validity of a signature on a document such as a contract or a will or can judge if a corporation is complying with terms of a liability settlement.

Forensic science also benefits the justice system in a somewhat unexpected way. Since reports produced by forensic scientists can show if a case has merit and should go to court, it can help to reduce the number of cases entering the overloaded court system.

To a certain degree, it might even be argued that forensic science has helped restore the public's faith in the legal system. The legal process as the means to justice was no longer a given for many people, based on the courts' inability to convict guilty parties and the incorrect convictions of innocent people. Today, with DNA technology and advances in other related areas, the forensic scientist can help present the facts in a criminal or civil case without depending on circumstantial evidence or unreliable witness testimony.

Although gathering and examining forensic evidence plays perhaps the largest role, there is much more to forensics than just DNA matching.

Forensic Science Fields

For further clarification, let's look at the different types of evidence as well as the definitions for other specific fields. Each of these topics is discussed in more detail in subsequent chapters.

- **Forensic evidence.** Forensic scientists and experts (also known as *criminalists*) work in the following areas (Chapter 2):

    Computer and digital image enhancement
    Crime scene reconstruction
    DNA
    Documents
    Drugs
    Entomology
    Fingerprints
    Firearms-ballistics
    Footwear and shoeprints
    Hair fibers
    Handwriting

Linguistics/audio
Locks
Paint
Photography
Poisons and other toxins
Polygraphs
Sculpting
Tire tracks and skid marks
Toolmarks
Voice and speech analysis

- **Forensic accident investigation.** Experts reconstruct accidents for testimony in law cases (Chapter 3).
- **Forensic pathology.** Pathology is the study of disease; forensic pathologists acquire additional training to apply the principles of pathology and of medicine in general to legal issues. They perform autopsies and conduct other investigations (Chapter 4).
- **Forensic death (medical or legal) investigation.** Also known as *coroners*, these investigators gather evidence and/or conduct autopsies for information to be used in the court system (Chapter 4).
- **Forensic medicine.** This field deals with the application of medical knowledge to questions of civil and criminal law, especially in court proceedings (Chapter 4).
- **Forensic odontology.** This is a branch of dentistry that deals with the collection, evaluation, and proper handling of dental evidence to assist in civil and criminal proceedings (Chapter 4).
- **Forensic nursing.** Forensic nurses work in both crime scene investigations and in settings such as rape crisis centers. They often work with forensic social workers (Chapter 4).

• **Forensic anthropology.** These artists and sculptors use their expertise to create reconstructions that can help identify remains or assailants (Chapter 5).

• **Forensic psychology and psychiatry.** This field involves the application of the related professions of psychology and psychiatry to questions and issues pertaining to law and the legal system. These scientists can help determine if a suspect is competent to stand trial or knew the difference between right and wrong when committing a crime (Chapter 6). Forensic social workers, psychiatric technicians, mental health workers, and counselors work with offenders within the criminal justice system (Chapter 6).

Other Forensic Disciplines

In addition to the established specialties just mentioned, the past several years have seen an increase in new areas of forensic study, many made possible by advances in technology.

• **Forensic computer examination.** Experts in this field are trained to locate and recover information from computers in a manner that is admissible in court. They may be consulted in cases ranging from fraud to pornography.

• **Forensic accounting.** Forensic accountants are experts who study white-collar crime such as fraud, embezzlement, or tax evasion using accounting techniques to determine the patterns of people who might have committed such crimes.

• **Forensic economics.** Forensic economists estimate the value of a victim's present and future lost income resulting from wrongful injury or death.

• **Wildlife forensics.** This specialty covers two main areas: identifying evidence; and linking the suspects, victims, and the crime scene by means of physical evidence. Experts determine poaching violations and work with state and federal officials to develop hunting regulations. They also enforce the Endangered Species Act. Wildlife forensics differs from criminal science only in that the victim (and occasionally the perpetrator) is an animal.

• **Forensic engineering.** Forensic engineers work on legal-related matters such as the quality evaluation of construction or manufacturing, failure analysis, and maintenance procedures. They examine structures ranging from apartment buildings or bridges to surgical implants or bones. Their expertise is applied in personal injury cases; construction, contract, or warranty disputes; patent or copyright infringements; and criminal and regulatory matters. Their work may overlap with that of accident and arson investigators.

• **Forensic architecture.** Forensic architects investigate construction defects and code violations for evidence to be used in a court of law. Their role can sometimes overlap the role of the forensic engineer.

Other forensic specializations include forensic administration, research, rehabilitation, laboratory investigation, field investigation, communications, and forensic education.

Forensic Science and the Law

Since law is at the core of forensics, lawyers work hand in hand with forensic scientists to advance the search for truth.

In addition to his or her own discipline, a successful forensics expert must also be an expert in communicating findings in legal proceedings. Even the most accurate findings are useless if the specialist can't communicate them in a clear fashion, whether to the law firm that requested them or to a jury in a court of law.

There are strict laws governing the collection, preservation, and admissibility of evidence, and a forensic specialist must know and conform to all of them. Failure to do so can cause an investigation to be tainted and may affect the outcome of a case.

Lawyers who use expert testimony in their work should have a better than basic knowledge of all the forensic sciences and must be articulate in presenting the findings of their expert witnesses. No matter how qualified the witness may be and however accurate the analysis of the evidence, the value of these tests and analyses will be diminished if the lawyer is untrained in the field and is unprepared to present the evidence effectively.

Sample Job Titles

Positions for forensic scientists come with a variety of job titles. Some employers might designate entry-level jobs with different levels, for example, forensic scientist I or forensic pathologist II. Other titles include but are not limited to the following:

Administrator of public services
Assistant medical examiner
Chemist
Criminalist
Deputy medical examiner
Director of laboratories
Document examiner
Drug chemist

Firearms examiner
Forensic chemist
Forensic consultant
Forensic DNA analyst
Forensic drug analyst associate
Forensic pathologist
Forensic scientist (DNA/trace evidence)
Forensic technologist
Histologist
Latent fingerprint examiner
Medical examiner
Odontologist
Professor (assistant, associate, or full)
Tool-mark examiner
Toxicologist
Trace analyst
Trace evidence technologist

Training

As you have seen, *forensic science* is a general term that encompasses a broad range of disciplines and levels of expertise. For example, a forensic scientist could be trained at the bachelor's level in toxicology, DNA, or ballistics. A forensic scientist could also be a Ph.D. psychologist who studies criminal behavior, profiles criminal suspects, and presents testimony in court; or he or she could be a Ph.D. forensic anthropologist who specializes in reconstructing skulls to identify remains.

The type of training you'll need to work as a forensic scientist will depend on your area of interest and the number of years you are willing to invest. If you plan to work mainly as a criminalist, specializing in one or more areas of forensic evidence (DNA or handwriting analysis, for example), you should earn a bachelor's degree and perhaps pursue graduate-level training. To work in one of the forensic medicine specialties, you would in most cases need a medical degree.

A valuable resource is offered by the American Academy of Forensic Sciences (AAFS). The Young Forensic Scientists Forum (YFSF) promotes the education and development of new forensic scientists. The YFSF is a way for beginning forensic scientists to interact with established practitioners in their field through meetings and educational sessions at the annual AAFS conference, a newsletter, and a mentorship program. Visit the "resources" link at the AAFS website for information at www.aafs.org.

Many graduates use an undergraduate degree in forensic science as a stepping-stone to graduate work in areas such as law, allied health and medicine, and engineering, to name a few.

You should keep in mind that a good number of forensic scientists don't necessarily start their careers working in forensics. For example, a psychologist might earn a Ph.D. in clinical psychology and then find that opportunities for consulting and other forensic work may develop into a full-time career. This can also happen for accident investigators, fire safety officers, or physical anthropologists, who find themselves becoming increasingly involved with forensic work that eventually replaces their original full-time career focus.

You will find specific training requirements for the different forensic specialties in the chapters that follow. Here are two examples of undergraduate and graduate programs in the field of forensic science.

Sample Programs

The two schools whose programs are profiled here are offered solely as examples of what you can expect in a forensic science program. Carefully consider all possibilities before selecting a specific school.

John Jay College of Criminal Justice
445 West 59th Street
New York, NY 10019
http://jjay.cuny.edu

John Jay College offers the bachelor of arts or bachelor of science degree in the following fields, which focus on criminal justice, fire science, and related areas of public service: computer information systems, correctional studies, criminal justice, criminal justice administration and planning, criminology, deviant behavior and social control, fire science, fire service administration, forensic psychology, forensic science government, judicial studies, justice studies, legal studies, police studies, public administration, and security management.

John Jay's bachelor of science in forensic science trains students who are seeking to work in forensic science laboratories or who are planning to pursue careers as scientists or scientist-administrators. The major draws primarily from chemistry (organic, analytical, and physical) with courses in biology, physics, and law. Students may specialize in one of three tracks: criminalistics, toxicology, or molecular biology. For the first three years, the following courses are required; seventy credits are needed to graduate:

Required Courses
Freshmen: Modern Biology
                        General Chemistry

Sophomores: Organic Chemistry
                     Quantitative Analysis
                     Law and Evidence
                     General Physics
Juniors: Physical Chemistry II
                     Biochemistry
                     Instrumental Analysis I and II

Criminalistics Track
Juniors: An Introduction to Criminalistics
Seniors: Forensic Science Laboratory
                     Internship
                     Forensic Science Laboratory

Toxicology Track
Juniors: Toxicology of Environmental
                     and Industrial Agents
Seniors: Forensic Science Laboratory
                     Internship
                     Forensic Pharmacology
                     Analytical Toxicology

Molecular Biology Track
Juniors: Genetics
Seniors: Forensic Science Laboratory
                     Internship
                     Molecular Biology I
                     Molecular Biology II

Master's programs offered at John Jay College of Criminal Justice include the following:

Master of Arts in Criminal Justice
Master of Public Administration
Master of Public Administration–Inspector General
    Program
Master of Science in Forensic Computing
Master of Arts in Forensic Psychology
Master of Science in Forensic Science
Master of Science in Protection Management

These master's programs complement baccalaureate degree study and may lead to doctoral study. The programs also provide for an opportunity to pursue new areas of specialization and are designed to meet the educational needs of pre-career, in-career, and in some cases, second-career students.

The City University of New York offers two doctoral programs at John Jay College in criminal justice and forensic psychology. The programs, which are administered by the Graduate School and the University Center of The City University of New York, prepare students for teaching, research, and policy development careers.

Virginia Commonwealth University
816 West Franklin Avenue
Richmond, VA 23284
www.vcu.edu

Virginia Commonwealth University offers a bachelor of science in forensic science with emphasis in biology, chemistry, and criminal justice. The Department of Forensic Science provides students with fundamental learning in forensic laboratory analyses and crime scene investigation. The program offers two tracks: forensic chemistry and forensic biology. To graduate, students need 122 credits.

Forensic Chemistry Track

Freshmen:	Introduction to Biological Science I and II
	Introduction to Biological Science Laboratory I and II
	General Chemistry
	General Chemistry Laboratory I and II
	Introduction to Life Sciences
	Calculus with Analytic Geometry
	Focused Inquiry I and II
Sophomores:	Organic Chemistry
	Organic Chemistry Laboratory I and II
	Justice System Survey or Policing Theories and Practice
	Writing and Rhetoric Workshop II
	General Physics
Juniors:	Physical Chemistry and Laboratory I
	Quantitative Analysis and Laboratory
	Scientific Crime Scene Investigation
	Survey of Forensic Science
	Forensic Evidence, Law, and Criminal Procedure
Seniors:	Instrumental Analysis and Laboratory
	Forensic Microscopy
	Forensic Chemistry

Professional Practices in Forensic
Science
Basic Practice of Statistics

Forensic Biology Track

Freshmen:
General Chemistry
General Chemistry Laboratory I
and II
Introduction to Life Sciences
Calculus with Analytic
Geometry
Basic Practice of Statistics
Focused Inquiry I and II

Sophomores:
Introduction to Biological Science I
and II
Introduction to Biological Science
Laboratory I and II
Writing and Rhetoric Workshop II
General Physics

Juniors:
Cell Biology
Biotechniques Laboratory
Genetics
Organic Chemistry
Organic Chemistry Laboratory I
and II
Scientific Crime Scene Investigation
Survey of Forensic Science
Forensic Microscopy
Forensic Evidence, Law, and
Criminal Procedures

Seniors:	Biochemistry
	Forensic Serology
	Forensic Molecular Biology
	Forensic Molecular Biology Laboratory
	Professional Practices in Forensic Science
	Forensic science or natural science elective

The master of science in forensic science degree requires thirty-six semester hours of course work, including twenty-four hours of required core course work and twelve hours of specialized course work designed for each track. The graduate program is a full-time, two-year program. Courses will vary depending on the track selected. Tracks offered include forensic biology, forensic chemistry/drugs and toxicology, forensic chemistry/trace, and the forensic physical track.

Most university departments of forensic science strongly encourage students who have no previous forensic science or criminal justice experience to participate in one or more internships in a criminal justice agency or forensic science laboratory. While most of these internships are almost always unpaid, they can provide valuable experience and a foot in the door when it comes time to land full-time employment.

Job Settings

Forensic scientists are employed by federal, state, provincial, and local governments and agencies. Some work for private laboratories; others work for universities. Still others work in hospitals and clinics or in private practice.

Self-employed forensic specialists might work in accident reconstruction, computer data recovery, or digital image-enhancing technology. The range of settings is as wide as the range of specialties.

If you plan to teach the forensic sciences, you will need the same education qualifications as instructors in any other field. Most university teaching jobs require a graduate degree. A master's degree is sufficient in some settings, but most professors must have a Ph.D. In addition to teaching experience, many positions also require field experience, especially for the more practical, hands-on types of courses.

Some university professors work in the field full-time or as part-time consultants while also teaching part-time.

Working Conditions

Working conditions for forensic scientists vary depending on the discipline and job setting. Those who work in laboratories or office settings generally have standard shifts and work in a comfortable environment. Specialists working in accident reconstruction, arson investigation, or crime scene investigation, to name just a few, must perform their duties in any setting, regardless of weather conditions or other physical discomforts.

In addition, the nature of crimes can be physically and emotionally disturbing. Those who work with crime victims, from the crime scene investigator to the medical examiner, must be prepared to encounter even the most unanticipated degree of physical trauma.

Salaries for Forensic Scientists

Salaries in this diverse field vary depending on the job title, level of expertise, employer, and geographic area.

As a general rule, federal agencies pay the most and local law enforcement agencies the least. Starting salaries could range from $30,000 per year to $45,000 per year, depending on the graduate's area of specialization and skills. Forensic experts with impressive credentials and many years of experience can command substantially more money.

The chapters ahead feature several firsthand accounts of forensic specialists working in the actual fields. Some provide salary information for their specific jobs.

2

FORENSIC EVIDENCE

THE RANGE OF evidence that might be found at a crime scene is enormous and requires the expertise of a team of forensic specialists working in collaboration to help solve the crime.

Evidence may be as microscopic as a flake of dried paint or a strand of hair or as large as the fuselage of an airplane found at the scene. It could be as subtle as an unlocked door or as obvious as a blood-covered knife lying next to a body.

Forensic evidence provides the largest arena in which *forensic scientists*, also known as *criminalists*, can show their expertise. Because the range of evidence is so vast, criminalists and forensic scientists often specialize in one or two areas. However, some specialists, especially those working in labs, must master more than one area.

Regardless of their specialty, all forensic scientists must be able to examine, analyze, identify, and interpret a range of physical evidence. They must be able to apply the techniques of the physical and natural sciences while examining evidence, with the end goal of proving the existence of a crime or connecting suspects to the crime. In many cases, they also must present their findings in a court of law. The information the forensic scientist collects is provided to investigators, attorneys, judges, and juries.

Crime Scene Reconstruction

A criminalist must be able to interpret results and findings to determine the circumstances at the time a crime occurred or perhaps to support a statement made by a witness.

Reconstructing the events of a crime can be very difficult. Criminalists use scientific methods, physical evidence, and deductive and inductive reasoning to gain knowledge of the events surrounding the commission of a crime. They also have to understand human behavior and the physical laws and processes involved in the crime.

All forensic findings must be conveyed to the other branches of the criminal justice system. This is usually done through written reports or expert testimony, and the criminalist must express conclusions so that technical details are understood by court and jury.

Specializations

A team of criminalists and forensic scientists study the scene of a crime to gather information and evidence. Some examples of their findings include the following:

- A chip of paint from a car is found on the clothing of a hit-and-run victim. Analysis of the paint leads to identification of the make of car.
- Skin particles are found under the fingernails of an assault victim. DNA analysis matches them to the DNA of a suspect.

- Ballistics testing proves that a bullet fired into a homicide victim does not come from a gun owned by a suspect.

- A blood spatter pattern appears confusing, with tiny marks along the floor, wall, and ceiling. A forensic entomologist proves that insects disturbed the crime scene and tracked blood in different places.

These are just a few examples of how forensic scientists help prove how a crime did—or didn't—happen.

Forensic scientists study hair, fibers, blood and semen stains, alcohol, drugs, paint, glass, botanicals, soil, flammable gases, and insulating materials. They must be able to restore smears or smudged markings, to identify or compare firearms and bullets, and to identify tool markings and shoeprints.

In this chapter we will examine more fully the areas of forensic photography and image enhancement, questioned documents/handwriting examination, toxicology and drug analysis, and trace evidence (hair, paint, fibers).

Forensic Photography and Image Enhancement

Forensic photographers are generally employed by police departments, medical examiners, sheriff's offices, and related law enforcement agencies. Their primary duty is to photograph evidence, document crime scenes, and operate the photo lab and darkroom.

Many law enforcement agencies have changed this job title to *imaging specialist* or *digital image enhancement specialist* because of the increasing use of digital technologies in addition to traditional photography.

Digital technology has been widely used in forensics since the 1990s. It is employed by police agencies as well as district attorneys and defense attorneys to enhance a fingerprint or videotape, an x-ray, or an audiotape. Digital imaging firms, such as Imaging Forensics (see the owner's firsthand account later in this chapter), also use digital imaging technology to create dynamic courtroom presentations.

Such firms and some forensic science programs offer training in digital imaging. Many police agencies that employ forensic photographers provide on-the-job training.

Questioned Documents

Document examiners answer questions regarding authorship, authenticity, alterations, additions, and erasures to documents such as wills, contracts, anonymous notes, deeds, medical records, income tax records, time sheets, contracts, loan agreements, election petitions, checks, and other documents.

They also deal with handwriting, typewriting, computer printing, the authenticity of signatures, photocopying processes, writing instruments, sequence of writing, and other elements of a document in relation to its authenticity.

A document examiner also may be called on to determine the significance of inks, paper, writing instruments, business machines, and other features of documents.

Forensic document examiners prepare reports of their findings and must often testify in court as expert witnesses. Questioned document courses are offered as part of criminal justice, police science, or forensic science college-level programs.

Some forensic document examiners are trained on the job, and some employers sponsor outside training. A bachelor's degree is required for this position. Training includes a two-year apprenticeship under the supervision of a court-qualified examiner, allowing a trainee to study the leading texts pertaining to questioned documents, perform supervised casework, prepare court exhibits, and conduct independent research. Some examiners work privately and may be found in most major cities.

Document examiners are typically employed by large police departments as well as most state and federal law enforcement agencies. Some of the most notable agencies include the Federal Bureau of Investigation; the Royal Canadian Mounted Police; the U.S. Secret Service; the U.S. Citizenship and Immigration Services; the U.S. Postal Inspection Service; the Internal Revenue Service; Revenue Canada—Customs, Excise, and Taxation; and the U.S. Army Crime Laboratory.

Many qualified examiners are members of the American Academy of Forensic Sciences and the American Society of Questioned Document Examiners. Many are certified by the American Board of Forensic Document Examiners, which is the only body that certifies these criminalists. The board aims to safeguard the public interest by ensuring that anyone who claims to be a specialist in forensic document examination does, in fact, possess the necessary skills and qualifications.

Applicants for certification must be engaged in the full-time practice of forensic document examination (exceptions are evaluated on an individual basis). They must also take comprehensive written, practical, and oral examinations that are based on a wide range of problems frequently encountered in document examination.

For more details about qualifying for certification, contact the American Board of Forensic Document Examiners. Contact information is provided in the Appendix.

Toxicology and Drug Analysis

Toxicology is the study of the harmful effects of chemicals, drugs, or poisons on living systems. Toxicologists pay particular attention to the conditions under which the harmful effects occur. *Forensic toxicology* refers to the interpretation of findings as they apply to the law. These findings often are used in a court of law to assist the judge or jury in making a decision.

There are three additional definitions for forensic toxicology: human-performance forensic toxicology, postmortem forensic toxicology, and forensic urine drug testing. Human-performance forensic toxicology determines the presence or absence of ethanol and other drugs and chemicals in blood, breath, or other appropriate specimens and evaluates their role in modifying human performance or behavior. One of the most common uses of this testing is to determine if someone was driving while intoxicated.

Postmortem forensic toxicology determines the presence or absence of drugs and their metabolites, chemicals such as ethanol and other volatile substances, carbon monoxide and other gases, metals, and other toxic chemicals in human fluids and tissues, evaluating their role as a determinant or contributory factor in the cause and manner of death.

Forensic urine drug testing determines the presence or absence of drugs and their metabolites in urine to demonstrate prior use or abuse. This method of testing is commonly used by employers and social services agencies to determine drug use.

Advances in medicine and the recreational uses of drugs and alcohol make the role of toxicologists very important. For example, they may be asked to work with emergency room staff to determine the cause of a coma or to assist law enforcement officers in determining the cause of unsafe driving. They may also assist a medical examiner in determining the cause of death. Interpretation of the results often requires the joint effort of doctors, coroners, and forensic scientists.

As with other specialties, training comes from extensive study in bachelor's-level forensic science or criminalistics programs, bachelor's-level chemistry programs, and, to some extent, on-the-job training.

Trace and DNA Evidence

Trace evidence refers to hair, fiber, paint/polymer, and glass, and it can also include gunshot residue. Trace and DNA evidence experts must possess a bachelor's degree in chemistry, forensic science, biology, or biochemistry. They also must be familiar with the use of specialized equipment, including a variety of microscopes, and must know the proper collection (from the bodies of victims of violent crimes, from crime scenes, and from accidents, for example), examination, and documentation procedures of trace evidence samples.

Credentials for Criminalists

The American Board of Criminalistics (ABC) offers a certification program for qualified professionals. The program includes a general knowledge exam and specialty exams in the fields of forensic biology, drug analysis, fire debris analysis, and trace evidence examination. The three levels of certification are diplomate, fellow, and technical specialist. To find out more about the certification program, go to the ABC website at www.criminalistics.com.

Diplomate

Certification as a diplomate (D-ABC) is awarded to individuals with a B.S. or B.A. in a natural science and two years of forensic laboratory experience who successfully complete the General Knowledge Examination. This exam is the first segment of a comprehensive certification program leading to the fellow designation (for examiners specializing in drug analysis; forensic biology, including DNA; fire debris analysis; or certain trace evidence specialty areas) or the diplomate designation (for those not seeking fellow status, such as lab directors or supervisors, or where specialty examinations are not currently planned). Certification as a diplomate signifies that the analyst is qualified to supervise multidisciplinary examinations of physical evidence.

Fellow

To be certified as a fellow of the American Board of Criminalistics (F-ABC), one must successfully complete the General Knowledge Examination, the relevant specialty examination, and a proficiency test and must have a minimum of two years' experience in the specialty area. The specialty areas currently offered are forensic biology, drug analysis, fire debris analysis, and trace evidence. Certification as an ABC fellow signifies that the analyst is qualified to supervise multidisciplinary evidence examinations and to conduct examinations in the specialty area.

Technical Specialist

Certification as a technical specialist (S-ABC) is awarded to those who successfully complete a written examination. Prerequisites include a B.S. or B.A. in a natural science, two years experience, and successful completion of a proficiency test in the last twelve months. This certification signifies that the analyst is qualified to conduct examinations in the specific fields for which the certificate is granted. Technical specialist certifications are currently offered in the specialties of forensic drug analysis and forensic molecular biology.

Sample Jobs

The following sample job advertisements will give you a good idea of the qualifications needed, the responsibilities, and the salary levels that different job titles offer. When you are ready to look for employment, an Internet search should provide you with numerous available positions. (Note: All the job listings included throughout this book are meant to be viewed as samples only; consequently, hiring bodies and contact information are not provided.)

Firearm/Tool Mark Examiner

Sheriff's office seeks qualified professional to examine firearm and tool mark evidence related to criminal investigations. Duties include examining firearms for operational capabilities, characterizations and comparisons of ammunition components, gunshot residue/shot pattern analysis, tool mark examinations, serial number restorations, operation of the NIBIN/IBIS computer, interpretation of laboratory analyses and results, preparation of written reports, and the ability to testify as an expert witness.

Requirements include bachelor's degree in a natural or physical science, and three years' forensic laboratory experience as a firearm/tool mark examiner are preferred. Applicants must be able to successfully pass a background investigation, polygraph examination, and drug screening. Salary: $55,000 to $70,000.

Forensic Technician

Sheriff's office is seeking qualified candidates for the position of forensic technician for the agency's ASCLD/ISO accredited crime laboratory. Employees in this classification perform highly specialized technical and scientific work that requires the accurate completion of a variety of standardized analytical tests, examinations, and procedures that may be complex in nature but generally do not require interpretation of results.

Position is responsible for the preparation, labeling, inventory, and maintenance of chemicals and equipment to ensure and protect the integrity of the testing procedures.

Requirements include a bachelor's degree emphasizing course work in biology, chemistry, medical technology, or related science; with additional upper-level undergraduate course work in one of the following: biology, chemistry, or medical technology. Six months' prior experience in a laboratory environment and working knowledge of Microsoft Office are also required. Salary: $32,030 to $47,323.

Crime Scene Analyst I

Metropolitan police department needs individual to perform crime scene investigations, collect evidence, provide testimony in court, perform various laboratory examinations of evidence, and other duties as assigned. Analyst responds to the scene of field investigations to perform the technical investigation of criminal and noncriminal scenes related to the identification, documentation, collection, preservation, and utilization of physical evidence. Performs laboratory examinations of evidence, including specialized processing involving physical, chemical, optical, and digital techniques. Obtains nontestimonial evidence, including hairs, fibers, saliva, blood, and other items from victims, suspects, and dead bodies. Prepares digital composite likenesses for criminal investigations. Attends postmortem examinations to collect desired evidence. Performs aerial and forensic imagery, as assigned. Provides testimony on forensic investigation and laboratory techniques in legal and administrative hearings.

Requirements include a minimum of one-year full-time experience in crime scene investigation. Specific training in crime scene investigations, photography, fingerprinting, latent print development, or related skills. Current certification or obtain certification as a crime scene investigator (CSI) under the certification program of the International Association of Identification within the probationary period. Ability to successfully complete a polygraph examination, background investigation, and reference checks, as well as vision (including color blindness) and hearing tests. Two years of college (sixty semester credit hours or the equivalent) with a bachelor's degree preferred. Salary: $22.48 to $31.48 per hour.

Forensic Specialist Trainee

Position supports the police department by obtaining and managing physical evidence in criminal cases including photographing; obtaining, analyzing, and identifying prints; analyzing handwriting; gathering physical and trace evidence; preparing sketches of crime scenes; and other related technical duties as required in coordination with investigators. Will interpret and apply federal, state, city, and departmental laws, policies, and procedures and independently perform a full range of police evidence investigative activities when fully trained. Will provide written and verbal documentation for courtroom testimony.

Requirements for trainee-level include an HS/GED diploma and a minimum of two years' work experience in the criminal justice field or in a laboratory setting or a four-year degree. Specialist I requires meeting the requirements for a trainee, six month's of satisfactory work experience in a position equivalent to the forensic specialist trainee, and the satisfactory completion of the basic latent print course work, which meets International Association for Identification (IAI) standards. Specialist II requires two years' work experience equivalent to the forensic specialist I in the criminal justice field or a related laboratory setting, an HS/GED diploma, and the satisfactory completion of the intermediate and advanced latent print course work, which meets IAI standards. Specialist III requires a combination of experience and training sufficient to meet the IAI certification requirements for latent print examiner; requires possession of IAI latent print examiner certification; and the successful completion of the Secret Service questioned document course. Salary: $2,153 per month.

Identification Specialist III

Will perform laboratory work in carrying out technical evidence work with demonstrated expertise in evidence collection, chemical processing, photography, and latent fingerprint processing. The primary job assignment is to examine latent fingerprints. Work is performed under the general direction of a forensic services section manager.

Requirements include at least four years of progressive experience with general police identification work in a law enforcement agency; an associate degree or bachelor's degree in forensics, chemistry, or related field preferred. Salary: $25.77 to $36.09 per hour.

TenPrint Examiner

Responsibilities include identifying fingerprints by conducting a thorough examination, researching fingerprints and related files to make identifications; storing and retrieving criminal information using specialized computer applications; communicating with law enforcement agencies on matters relating to criminal information; and fingerprinting and photographing sex offenders as they register with the county sheriff's office.

Requirements include knowledge of laws, policies, and procedures pertaining to law enforcement and detention and data privacy regulations; knowledge of detention records system, warrant systems, Automated Fingerprint Identification System (AFIS), Live Scan fingerprint capture system, and computerized criminal history system; knowledge of current computerized technology for collecting, searching, and identifying fingerprints and taking photographs; skill in applying modern methods in comparing and making TenPrint identifications accurately; skill in using ink and computer scanning equipment to fingerprint individuals and produce quality photographic images; and skill in troubleshooting fingerprint computer hardware and software issues. Salary: $43,160 to $54,704.

Civilian Crime Scene Technician

Police department seeks civilian crime scene technician to oversee complex crime scene investigations, including but not limited to homicides, sexual assaults, armed robberies, home invasions, and property crimes such as burglaries. Duties include processing crime scenes, packaging and transporting evidence, attending and photographing autopsies, and attending briefings and conferences with the police agencies requesting assistance. Technician will prepare investigative reports, testify in court, receive continuing education, instruct classes, and maintain equipment in a state of readiness. Maintains an in-depth knowledge of federal and state statutes, court cases related to work performed, and agency rules and regulations.

Requirements include an associates degree in physical science, law enforcement, photography, criminal/forensic sciences, or a closely related field or two years' experience in law enforcement, security, advanced photography, or a closely related field or equivalent combination of education and experience. Salary: $2,940 to $3,855 per month.

Crime Scene Technician

This is a civilian position assisting sworn officers assigned to the investigation of criminal cases. Work involves collection and preservation of physical evidence found at crime scenes; fingerprint processing and analysis; photography; physical evidence examination and analysis in cooperation with sworn officers assigned to the investigation of criminal cases; packaging, preserving, and storing evidence; maintaining the chain of custody; and presenting court testimony as an expert witness in regard to physical evidence. Work is performed under the general supervision of the unit commander on a formal work schedule, which includes callback on a rotating basis.

Requirements include an associates degree in criminal justice in forensic science, criminalistics, biology, chemistry, criminal justice, or related field from an accredited technical institute or community/junior college. One year of experience in police-related work including forensics, fingerprint, processing, and collection procedures. Salary: $30,812 to $46,443.

Evidence/ID Specialist

The primary responsibly of this position is to perform specialized work in the investigation of crime scenes, and the identification of victims and suspects for the city's police department.

Requirements include knowledge of forensic science methods and standards; techniques used in print processing, bloodstain pattern analysis, and crime scene procedures; trace evidence collection procedures; forensic imaging software; and police policies and procedures. Must be skilled in evidence collection and crime scene investigation, fingerprint collection, and identification of print pattern matches. Must possess exceptional oral, written, interpersonal, and time management skills; be detail-oriented; and have demonstrated the ability to prepare reports. Salary: $34,561 to $51,842.

Firearms Technical Lead

This position will be responsible for ensuring proper quality assurance and quality control measures relevant to firearms. This includes documentation, instrument calibration, and maintenance logs; reviewing relevant casework; maintaining the NIBIN database; continuous evaluation of methods employed including an annual review of standard operating procedures and proposing new and/or modified analytical procedures to be used by the analysts. In addition, the firearms technical leader is required to perform routine and more difficult firearms case assignments, both in the laboratory and in the field.

Requirements include experience as a firearms examiner dedicated to staying abreast of changes within the industry as well as a sound technical advisor and trainer who fosters teamwork and cooperation. Applicants who are active participants in the Association of Firearms and Toolmarks Examiners (AFTE) and who have pursued or are in the process of pursuing AFTE certification as a firearms examiner are strongly desired. Salary: $6,789 to $8,488 per month.

Firsthand Accounts

Read the following accounts of forensic science professionals to see what this interesting work is really like.

Sandra Ramsey Lines, Forensic Document Examiner

A former government examiner, Sandra Ramsey Lines is now in private practice based in Arizona. Her clients come from all over the country.

She earned an A.A. in criminal justice from Scottsdale Community College and a B.A. in management from the University of

Phoenix. Her career began with a two-year internship with the Arizona Department of Public Safety.

Getting Started

While employed as a police officer/detective with the Cleveland Police Department in Ohio, Sandra was in charge of a complicated investigation involving fraudulent checks. She was so impressed with the examiner and his work that she decided to enter the field. The examiner offered to train two Cleveland police officers in a two-year program, and since Sandra didn't have a degree, she put in a request to join the program, but it was not acted upon at that time. Although she loved her work as a law enforcement officer, she never lost interest in questioned document work, so when the opportunity came along years later in Arizona, she took it.

While employed as a special agent with the attorney general's office of Arizona, Sandra worked with an assistant attorney general with whom she shared a recognition of the need for more qualified document examiners. They were able to find a mentor with the state laboratory who agreed to conduct training and obtained a federal grant to pay Sandra's salary while she was in training. She eventually established the state's questioned document laboratory.

In 1996, a different attorney general decided to close the laboratory, which was 75 percent federally funded and served the Medicaid fraud units throughout the United States. She felt that she had a choice: to remain as a special agent with the agency and give up four difficult years of training, research, and certification preparation; or move to another agency. She retired as an Arizona law enforcement officer and became a senior forensic document examiner with the Bureau of Alcohol, Tobacco and Firearms in Walnut Creek, California. Two years later she returned to Arizona and started a private practice.

What the Work Is Like

Sandra explains that the examination of questioned documents is conducted by analyzing and comparing questioned handwriting, handprinting, typewriting, commercial printing, photocopies, papers, inks, and other documentary evidence with known materials to establish the authenticity of the contested (or questioned) material, as well as the detection of alterations.

The examiner assists lawyers and the courts by examining and offering written opinions on a variety of disputed document problems, including wills, deeds, medical records, income tax records, time sheets, contracts, loan agreements, election petitions, checks, and anonymous letters to determine identity, source, authenticity, alterations, additions, deletions, or other germane issues. In addition, a forensic document examiner (FDE) must give expert testimony and be prepared to demonstrate and support his or her findings to a court of law or regulatory body.

Recognition as a candidate for certification by the American Board of Forensic Document Examiners (ABFDE), the only board recognized by the American Academy of Forensic Sciences and the American Society of Questioned Document Examiners, requires a minimum of a bachelor's degree and successful completion of a minimum two-year, full-time training program in a qualified laboratory or with a qualified forensic document examiner (FDE) recognized by the board.

Sandra says that her work is never boring because each case is unique and presents its own challenges. One day she might work on a disputed will involving the possibility of forged signatures, typewriting identification, and paper insertions. The next day's case might involve an anonymous note involving a computer-generated document.

Because Sandra's findings may be responsible for sending someone to prison or helping someone prove his or her innocence, she keeps abreast of the latest research in her field, generally through continuing education. She conducts independent research, publishes in respected scientific journals, and remains active as a member of professional organizations.

Upsides and Downsides

Sandra derives satisfaction from discovering evidence that can lead to a definitive conclusion and knowing that she's done her job well. However, not all cases have definitive conclusions, and sometimes she must say that she doesn't know the answer conclusively. She must acknowledge her limitations and be prepared to consult colleagues with more experience or expertise in certain areas.

A qualified FDE must make every effort to be impartial and avoid mistakes. A serious error can cost an examiner's reputation and credibility in court.

FDEs in private practice must invest a considerable amount of money to obtain the proper equipment to conduct examinations. They must establish good credentials and a reputation for honesty with their clients. Sandra says, "My findings may not be what a client hopes for, but I must be willing to give the bad with the good."

Sandra finds that one downside of the work in both public and private practice is dealing with the attorneys who have hired (knowingly or unknowingly) nonqualified individuals who represent themselves as FDEs. Many of these people received their training in graphology (nonscientific reading of a subject's personality from his or her handwriting). Some purport to be certified by a board with a name similar to the American Board of Forensic Document

Examiners, but these other boards do not utilize the more stringent qualifications or testing requirements of the ABFDE. It can sometimes be difficult to explain these differences in an inoffensive manner to a lay jury.

Sandra says that in private practice another downside may be getting paid by clients; most examiners require a retainer prior to conducting examinations. Also, days may go by without any work, or there may be a sudden inundation of cases. A private examiner must be prepared for either situation.

Salaries

An FDE in government practice can earn from $35,000 to $90,000 a year, depending on his or her agency and credentials. In private practice, FDEs charge anywhere from $100 to $250 per hour, again depending on their location and what the market will bear or what their credentials are.

Advice from a Professional

Sandra cautions that it is difficult to obtain training as an FDE from a qualified examiner or accredited laboratory. She suggests earning a forensic science degree and then applying for any position in a government laboratory. From there you will have the opportunity to meet a qualified examiner and possibly obtain training.

George Reis, Forensic Digital Imaging Consultant

George Reis is the owner of Imaging Forensics, a digital imaging firm in Fountain Valley, California. He began his career as a forensic photographer and has been working in the field for nearly twenty years.

Getting Started

George has extensive experience as a photographer, with specializations in photojournalism and in advertising photography. He says that he chose the field of forensic photography purely by accident. He owned a struggling commercial photography business and decided to find a job in photography rather than continue the struggle. He saw a classified listing for a photographer with the Newport Beach Police Department and decided to apply, although he had never had an interest in this type of photography or in police work in general. He thought that he would work at the job temporarily but found it to be an incredible opportunity that led to his successful consulting/training business. He started the consulting business because he saw a strong need for someone to help other police agencies take advantage of digital imaging technology.

After working as a forensic photographer for a couple of years, George realized that many aspects of the job could be done better with digital imaging technology. He introduced these concepts to the agency where he worked and began sharing this with other agencies, eventually starting his own consulting business.

George has taken numerous courses offered through law enforcement and forensics-based organizations. These include classes in fingerprint identification methods, crime scene investigation, and educational conferences offered through the International Association for Identification (IAI), Evidence Photographers International Council (EPIC), American Academy of Forensic Science (AAFS), and others.

George counts himself among the six or eight early users of digital technology, and he has collaborated with others to develop many of the techniques used for digital image processing, including enhancement and analysis. He is the author of *Photoshop CS3 for Forensics Professionals: A Complete Digital Imaging Course for Investigators*, published by Sybex in 2007.

What the Work Is Like

George explains that forensic digital imaging is the legal use of photographs and images for documentation or analysis of crime scenes, evidence, or accident scenes. His job is unique because he is a business owner working directly with police agencies, investigative firms, and attorneys on casework.

As a digital imaging consultant, he works in three areas. The first is consulting, where he helps police and investigative agencies incorporate the use of digital imaging equipment. This includes recommending equipment, writing protocols, and configuring and installing equipment.

The second is training, which includes teaching forensic personnel how to use the hardware and software for digital imaging, as well as the legal requirements and digital technology theory.

The third is enhancement and analysis services, providing his services to agencies and businesses that may not have the expertise or equipment to do it themselves. This provides him with a lot of variations in his day-to-day work.

George occasionally travels to teach workshops in digital imaging or to consult with an agency on how they can implement the technology. At other times, he enhances videotapes or negatives to try to get the most information from these images.

As an example, he was given a videotape of a burglary in which the two suspects pulled up to a closed convenience store in a commercial truck, broke the glass in the front door to enter, took merchandise, and then exited with the goods. By enhancing the frames of the video that showed their truck through the store window,

George was able to positively identify the unique numbering on the cab of the truck. This led to an arrest, which then led to the identification and conviction of the two suspects.

Upsides and Downsides

George finds that the most exciting aspect of his work is seeing the excitement that others get from learning the technology. It is also fulfilling when a prosecutor or defense attorney tells him that his work made a significant difference in the case.

The most difficult part is traveling when he doesn't want to. Also, as a business owner, he is responsible for all the paperwork and tax information that must be kept up to date.

Salaries

George says that a forensic photographer earns from about 25 percent less than a police officer to about 10 percent more. This depends on the agency and whether there is a senior or supervisory position available. His income as a business owner is based on his volume of work. When he is busy, he earns more than a forensic photographer.

Advice from a Professional

"Get experience anywhere and everywhere you can," George recommends. He suggests volunteering at your local police department, studying photography, and also learning about software applications and signal processing. He also suggests joining organizations, such as the International Association for Identification and Electronic Primary Information Center, and attending their conferences and meetings.

A Final Thought

The field of forensic evidence offers many options for those interested in getting to the root of a crime. Whether you want to learn crime scene reconstruction, examine questioned documents, or specialize in toxicology or ballistics, you can build a career that allows you to work as part of a forensics team.

3

ACCIDENT AND
FIRE INVESTIGATION

IN 2005, 43,443 people died in motor vehicle crashes in the United States. In Canada, motor vehicle crashes claimed 9,100 lives. An additional 2.7 million Americans and 653,000 Canadians were injured.

According to the U.S. Department of Transportation and Transport Canada, motor vehicle accidents are the leading cause of death from ages one to thirty-four. Several factors contribute to these numbers, including speed, type of vehicle, road conditions, and the use of alcohol or drugs. Even an insect trapped in a car or a sudden fit of sneezing can contribute to these unfortunate statistics.

Although the number of alcohol-related fatalities has declined slightly, alcohol-impaired drivers still remain a major problem. In the United States, 16,885 deaths were attributed to alcohol consumption, and alcohol was a factor in 36 percent of Canadian motor vehicle deaths. About one-third of all motor vehicle deaths involve vehicles leaving the road and hitting trees or utility poles; alcohol is a contributing factor in many of these crashes.

The U.S. Fire Administration reports that in 2006 fires killed more Americans than all natural disasters combined. In addition to 106 firefighters killed while on duty, 3,245 civilians lost their lives as the result of fire, and another 16,400 were injured. Direct property loss due to fires was estimated at $11.3 billion.

The most recent data available from Statistics Canada indicate that in 2002, 304 civilians were killed in fires, and another 2,547 were injured. Property losses due to fires were estimated to be $1.5 billion.

Fires can start in seemingly countless ways. But whether it is a kitchen fire caused by sputtering oil or a devastating forest fire that claims millions of acres, they all fall into just two categories: accidental or criminal.

An accident happens when an unattended candle ignites a nearby curtain or when a worker inadvertently spills a flammable liquid near an open flame. On the other hand, criminal fires are set deliberately, with the intention of causing damage or even death. This is arson, and it is a very serious crime. Fires caused by bombs, understandably, also fall under the category of criminal fires.

In 2006, an estimated 31,000 intentionally set structure fires resulted in 305 civilian deaths in the United States and in an estimated $755 million in property damage. Arson accounted for more than 13,000 fires in Canada.

Some examples of arson are a fire set by a business owner who hopes to collect insurance money, an act of revenge against an enemy, or pure vandalism. There are several different motives for arson: spite, revenge, anger, and fraud. Solving arson crimes also can help shed light on other crimes because many arson fires are set to cover other criminal activity, such as dealings in illegal drugs.

Role of Investigators

Professional investigators are consulted when a traffic accident is believed to be the result of criminal negligence, such as driving while intoxicated, or when the origin of a fire is suspicious.

Police departments and prosecuting attorneys have their own traffic accident investigators, but criminal defendants can also hire independent investigators to help prove innocence. Regardless of which side of the case they are on, all traffic investigators work with the goal of uncovering the causes of the accident.

Traffic investigators examine the actual scene or study photographs and videos of the scene. If called in much after the fact, they try to re-create the scene using the techniques of accident reconstruction. They research and study conditions at the time of the accident, such as lighting, the weather, visibility, and any other factors that might have been a factor.

A forensic entomologist might even be asked to examine the fragmented remains of insects that have impacted and lodged on the front fascia, windshields, and radiators of automobiles. Analysis of such remains can yield evidence to the probable path of an automobile when pinpointing the location and areas of travel.

Fire investigators look into both accidental and criminal fires. Once the engine company has put out a fire, the lieutenant on the scene will try to determine how the fire started. If there appears to be substantial monetary loss, or there is a suspicion that the fire wasn't accidental, a fire investigator conducts a more in-depth check.

In the optimal situation, the fire investigator would be at the scene while the fire is still burning, because a fire in progress can reveal a lot of information. The color of the flame or the smoke can often indicate what caused the fire, and the way the fire reacts to water also gives clues. If the fire doesn't go right out when soaked, if it keeps coming back, then there's a good chance fuel was used.

Fire investigators also look at which part of the building is burning to try to determine where the fire started. After the fire has been extinguished, burn patterns in wood or carpeting also reveal clues.

Investigators study wiring, fuse boxes, and circuit breaker boxes. They interview the firefighters who arrived first on the scene and ask what they saw. Were the doors unlocked? Was anyone running away? Was there broken glass lying inside or was it blown outside by the fire?

Unfortunately, only a small percentage of arsonists are caught and convicted. But arsonists often like to mingle in the crowd of onlookers to watch the firefighters at work. Knowing this, some fire departments use "fire dogs"—accelerant detection canines—to sniff out gasoline or other accelerants at a fire scene. They are also taken through the crowd to uncover the arsonist, whose clothing might still have the smell of gasoline.

Both accident and arson investigators often must go to court and testify. Their expert opinions are highly regarded and may be the factor that determines innocence or guilt.

Training for Investigators

Courses for accident investigation and reconstruction are offered at community colleges, traffic safety institutes, and four-year colleges and universities that offer bachelor's degrees in the subject. The programs can come under a variety of names or departments: traffic safety, transportation, transportation engineering, accident investigation, and so on.

Most fire and arson investigators first go through regular firefighter training and put in their time as a firefighter. Once they receive departmental approval, they may begin the ongoing process of training to become investigators. Training includes attending special classes at colleges and fire academies and also completing internships with seasoned investigators. Their studies include fire behavior, chemistry, court procedures, and how to handle evidence.

Not all fire investigators work for fire departments. With the appropriate training and experience, some might find work with insurance companies or private investigation firms.

Northwestern University's Center for Public Safety offers an investigator-training program, profiled here.

Northwestern University
Center for Public Safety
1801 Maple Avenue
Evanston, IL 60208
www.nucps.northwestern.edu

The Center for Public Safety was established at Northwestern University as the Traffic Institute in 1936. The center is a national nonprofit organization that serves public agencies responsible for law enforcement, criminal justice, public safety, traffic management, and highway transportation systems. Local, county, state, and federal government agencies, as well as agencies from foreign countries, are served through programs of specialized training, continuing education, research and development, publications, and direct assistance.

In addition to the accident investigation division, the focus of our discussion here, the center maintains three other divisions: management training, safety and security, and transportation engineering.

The accident investigation division has a comprehensive curriculum. It provides consulting services and expert-witness testimony and also acts as a clearinghouse in distributing accident investigation and reconstruction information to police agencies, prosecutors, and others in the public and private sectors. Following are examples of the courses offered by the Center for Public Safety's Accident Investigation division.

- **Accident Investigation 1 and 2.** These courses offer an in-depth study of the skills needed to investigate a traffic accident by recognizing, preserving, and recording critical evidence at the accident scene. Students will learn to make measurements, sketches, and after-accident diagrams and to photograph the accident scene. Use of the collected data in accident reconstruction is also covered.
- **Basic Physics and Mathematics Workshop.** This course reviews mathematics and elementary physics used in traffic accident reconstruction. It is designed as a refresher course for the student who has studied these concepts in the past but may have not used them for years. Students will find this course valuable in building a foundation for accepted theories in accident reconstruction courses.
- **Vehicle Dynamics.** Dynamics is the branch of mechanics that deals with the motion of bodies and the action of forces in producing or changing that motion. Vehicle Dynamics covers the dynamics relating to motor vehicle accidents. After successfully completing this course, students will have been introduced to the basic mathematical procedures necessary for attending Traffic Acci-

dent Reconstruction 1 and 2. This course involves a considerable amount of physics and mathematics. Prospective students should have successfully completed a high school physics course as well as high school–level algebra, geometry, and trigonometry. To ensure that applicants have the proper math background, admission will be based on the results of a mathematics-screening exam sent to each applicant and graded by NUCPS staff. Applicants who are uncertain about their mathematical skills should plan on attending the Basic Physics and Mathematics Workshop.

• **Traffic Accident Reconstruction 1 and 2.** Accident reconstruction focuses on analyzing and interpreting information that has already been collected at lower levels of investigation. Students will learn the skills needed to determine how an accident occurred. The objective is to describe the accident in as much detail as possible. Through lectures, course material, and the analysis of real-world case studies, students will be provided with the training needed to successfully reconstruct traffic crashes. Participants must possess skills normally learned during on-scene and technical accident investigation training (Accident Investigation 1 and 2) and improved with experience. These skills include the ability to prepare after-accident situation maps and classify and interpret vehicle damage, properly interpret marks on the road, and be proficient in algebra.

• **Heavy Vehicle Crash Reconstruction.** This course includes four hours of field testing to demonstrate various braking and acceleration characteristics of heavy vehicles and to allow students the chance to analyze and apply the collected data. It also covers case studies showing how various analytic techniques can be applied to real world accidents. Students will review each case study and discuss how it relates to an actual situation.

• **Pedestrian Vehicle Traffic Collisions.** This course stresses the importance of accuracy in investigating and reconstructing accidents involving pedestrians. Students will learn the mathematical equations for kinematics of bodies and what formulas are appropriate for which scenario.

Salaries

Accident investigators employed by police departments or other government agencies are generally paid on the same scale as other personnel. The salary would vary depending on the geographic region and the agency's budget. Beginning investigators have starting salaries between $32,000 and $45,000 and move up with more experience.

Accident investigators and reconstructionists working privately most often charge by the hour, anywhere from $100 to $200 per hour.

Median annual earnings of firefighters are about $38,330 nationwide. Firefighting and prevention supervisors average about $58,920. Median annual earnings of fire inspection occupations are about $46,340; those employed by local governments average $48,020.

Firefighters who average more than a certain number of hours a week are required to be paid overtime. The hours threshold is determined by the department during the firefighter's work period, which ranges from seven to twenty-eight days. Firefighters often earn overtime for working extra shifts to maintain minimum staffing levels or for special emergencies.

Generally speaking, fire and arson investigators who work for insurance companies are paid slightly higher than those who work for fire departments.

Sample Jobs

The following sample job advertisements will give you an idea of the qualifications needed, the responsibilities, and the salary levels that different job titles offer. When you are ready to look for employment, an Internet search should provide you with numerous available positions.

Forensic Chemist I

The Drug Enforcement Administration is seeking applicants for the position of Forensic Chemist. Responsibilities: Performs analyses on drug evidence and interprets data to detect, identify, and quantitate controlled substances. Determines the identity and/or concentration of adulterants and diluents, which meet established thresholds. Renders expert testimony on own work in federal, state, or local courts. Assists prosecuting attorneys in the preparation of technical aspects of a case. As directed or requested, provides advice and/or assistance in the performance of enforcement activities such as clandestine laboratory seizures and vacuum-sweep searches for controlled substances. Writes laboratory reports that describe all tests performed, calculations, and conclusions.

Requirements include a bachelor's or higher degree in physical sciences, life sciences, or engineering that included 30 semester hours in chemistry, supplemented by course work in mathematics through differential and integral calculus, and at least 6 semester hours of physics. Ability to communicate effectively other than in writing; ability to communicate in writing; skill in interpreting and applying guidelines, policies, and procedures; knowledge of chemistry principles, theories, and practices; knowledge of laboratory methods, procedures, and techniques used in analytical chemistry; ability to operate and calibrate common laboratory instruments; ability to collaborate with others to carry out routine work, scientific research, projects, or studies. Salary: $25,623 to $113,438.

Police and Fire Criminalist III

Performs advanced analyses in connection with the identification and comparison of objects and materials in a crime laboratory and performs related administrative and supervisory assignments. May train Criminalists I and II in advanced casework and legal aspects of evidence evaluation and may execute administrative duties over one or more laboratory sections as assigned.

Requires three years of experience at a journey level in a criminalistic laboratory and a bachelor's degree in chemistry, criminalistics, or a related field. Requires knowledge of principles, methods, materials, equipment, and current techniques of criminalistics. Also requires general competency in at least ten (10) major criminalistic areas OR a master level of competency in one major criminalistic area. The 12 criminalistic areas are:

1. Analytical chemistry
2. Drug identification,
3. Blood alcohol
4. Forensic blood testing
5. Hair and fiber identification
6. Arson investigation
7. Polarized microscopy
8. Firearms and tool-marks identification
9. Toxicology
10. General comparative analysis,
11. Technical macrophotography and photomicrography
12. X-ray techniques

Other experience and education that meet the minimum requirements may be substituted. Salary: $53,976 to $76,544.

Firsthand Accounts

The following accounts from professional investigators will give you an inside look at this aspect of forensic science.

Jack Murray, Accident Investigator

Jack Murray is a certified legal investigator and accident reconstructionist. He has a bachelor's degree from the University of Hartford in Connecticut and an M.B.A. from the University of Connecticut in Storrs. He has also attended more than thirty-five specialized investigative seminars in accident investigation and reconstruction, including accident reconstruction (Texas A&M University) and accident photography and DWI/vehicular homicide (both at the Northwestern University Center for Public Safety).

Jack has been named one of the top five investigators in America by *PI Magazine* and one of the top twenty-five investigators of the century by the National Association of Investigative Specialists. He has received a lifetime achievement award from the National Association of Investigative Specialists, and in 2003 he received the NAIS author of the year award. In 2004 he was the winner of the R. K. Hakanson award from the Evidence Photographers International Council for his contributions to the field of evidence photography. He is the author of seven books on the subject and is internationally recognized as expert lecturer and teacher. He has been doing investigative work in this field since 1976 and accident reconstruction work since 1984. He started specializing in criminal defense of vehicular crime in 1989.

Jack is a former regional director of the National Association of Legal Investigators and former president of the North Texas Private Investigators Association.

Getting Started

Jack took a job on Wall Street after getting his M.B.A. Although he didn't enjoy the work, he earned a substantial amount of money. However, a series of heart attacks at age twenty-eight made him realize that there were more important things in life than financial rewards.

He had worked as an insurance fire/arson investigator while attending college and decided that the investigative field might be interesting. He originally worked in criminal defense but became interested in accident investigation that applied the laws of physics and mathematics to motor vehicle accidents to determine the causes and effects of vehicle dynamics.

Jack decided to combine his criminal defense work with accident investigation and began to work on defense of vehicular crimes, such as manslaughter and criminally negligent homicide. The more involved he became in the field, the more he realized the importance of continuing education as a way to stay abreast of the computer and scientific applications used in the field.

He worked for an investigator from the Dallas County District Attorney's office, and then a few years later, when his boss moved to California, Jack inherited his clients. In 1976 he obtained his own license as a private investigator from the Texas Commission on Private Security. Jack realized the importance of forensic photography when he saw that many cases were won or lost based on photographs that were taken at the crime scene. Jack's work includes both civil and criminal cases. In both situations, he thoroughly investigates the circumstances and causes that led to an accident and determines if there was any criminal action or whether it is a civil situation. Jack finds the work extremely challenging, particularly because he seldom gets a case until well after it has occurred and, therefore, must work with photos, measurements, and statements taken by someone else, usually a police agency. He must reconstruct the scene based almost totally on information provided by others.

Upsides and Downsides

Jack experiences a great deal of satisfaction when he is able to help an innocent client avoid a jail sentence. He also appreciates his position as a high-profile professional who gets to work on some very big cases but acknowledges that it took a long time to build this reputation and to develop the skills that go with it.

He also likes the fact that the job is never boring and that every case is different. Each one brings a new client with his or her own characteristics and an attorney who usually determines how a case will be presented to a jury. If the attorney doesn't know how best to use the information Jack has provided, it's part of Jack's job to tactfully explain it.

Jack is occasionally frustrated by the disparity between the vast resources of the state and the limited resources of most defendants. He says, "Most times people only get as much justice as they can afford." Regardless of his clients' position in the community, it is his responsibility to provide them with the best defense possible.

The work requires frequent interaction with law enforcement personnel, which can also be difficult. Some officers are extremely professional and helpful, while others are less cooperative with investigators.

In addition, Jack occasionally finds that he can't help a client, when the results of his investigation or reconstruction reveal that the facts are not in the client's favor. This is news that clients do not want to hear, especially when they have paid a lot of money for his services.

Sample Cases

Jack recalls a case in which his client left a Christmas party and turned the wrong way onto a one-way street, where he collided head-on with another vehicle, killing the other driver. A blood test determined that the client was legally intoxicated, and he was charged with DWI manslaughter.

Although the state's case may have seemed solid, Jack was able to prove that the traffic signs were so confusing and poorly placed that even a sober driver could have made the same turn and had the same accident. The client was given five years' probation instead of fifteen years in the penitentiary.

Another client hit a parked car on the side of the road in a rainstorm, killing the driver, who was sitting in the parked vehicle. The client was charged with criminally negligent homicide. Jack produced a videotape under conditions similar to those at the accident scene, which he used in combination with still photos taken by the police at the scene. He was able to prove that the victim's parking lights were not on at the time of the accident, and that given the weather and lighting conditions, the client had insufficient time to recognize the parked car and either swerve or stop. The client was found not guilty.

Salaries

Jack says that although you won't gain instant recognition in the field, you can make a very good living after a relatively short period of time if you put enough effort into obtaining the necessary training and experience it takes to succeed. Because of the need to acquire experience, investigators generally start at relatively low wage levels.

A qualified reconstructionist usually charges between $150 and $250 per hour. An experienced accident investigator usually earns between $100 and $175 dollars per hour.

Some weeks you might work seventy hours on a case and the following week only five, so cash flow is sometimes very irregular, although most experienced investigators and/or reconstructionists receive a substantial retainer up front.

Advice from a Professional

Jack recommends asking your local police department if you can ride along with one of its accident investigators to get a feel for what the work is really like.

He also suggests asking local private sector experts if you can shadow them to see what the mechanics involve. Find your local investigative associations (every state has at least one) and attend some of their meetings to find out which members do this work.

For formal education, Jack advises a major in criminal justice, math, physics, or engineering, depending on your own aptitudes and interests. You might investigate one of the many community colleges that offer two-year programs in criminal justice. Adding a few extra courses in math or physics will put you in a good position to find a job at graduation.

Jack cautions that the job requires a lot of testifying under oath in depositions and trials, and the determination of who can qualify as an expert witness is made individually for each case. Qualifying as an expert in one case doesn't necessarily mean that you will be qualified to testify in another.

Robert Lemons, Fire Investigator

Robert (Bob) Lemons is a fire investigator with a South Florida fire department. He is also a trained firefighter and paramedic and the handler of Holly, an accelerant detection canine.

Getting Started

When he joined the fire department, Bob gained a broader view of what goes on in the department as a whole. And while he liked riding the rescue trucks, he found fire investigation more interesting. "I watched the investigators come in at a fire and I asked a lot of questions. 'Why are you doing this?' 'Why are you looking here?' 'What are you looking for?'"

Bob persisted in his curiosity, and his supervisors became aware of his interest in fire investigation.

Holly, the Accelerant Detection Canine

Bob read a magazine article about accelerant canines being used by fire investigators and told his chief that he would like to pursue investigation and work with a trained dog. He asked to be sent to the Maine State Police Canine Academy in Portland for five weeks with a dog to learn how to investigate fires.

Holly was a three-year-old Labrador donated by a local family and trained to search for residue of flammable liquids. Upon detection of a combustible substance, she signals Bob, and samples are collected and sent to a lab for examination. Detection of a substance doesn't always indicate arson, however. Many people store charcoal lighter fluid or gasoline for lawn mowers in the house or garage; either of these might be the cause of an accidental fire. Once Holly finds the fuel, it's up to the human fire investigators to take over and determine the nature of the fire.

Holly has been trained on a food reward system; the only time she eats is when she finds something. To maintain her schedule, on days off Bob uses drops of a specially prepared flammable liquid that Holly can "search" for at his home. She is fed once she finds the liquid. This is a strict routine with no deviations for treats.

Holly has actually helped to catch arsonists, who sometimes linger after a fire to watch the firefighters at work. Bob walks Holly through the crowd, and if she detects the scent of an accelerant on anyone, the police can arrest that person for suspected arson.

Upsides and Downsides

Bob enjoys the opportunity to interact with many people and different agencies, such as local police, the state fire marshal, and federal agents. And he always takes pleasure in working with Holly. "She's a good partner," he says. "But she has her moods, just like we do. There are days you don't feel like working, and the same holds true for Holly. Sometimes at fire scenes or—it will always be when it's important—at a demonstration for a fire official, Holly will just look around and say, 'Not today.' You can tell she's just going through the motions.

"The rewards of this job can be few and far between. Especially when you know how a fire started, know that it was arson, but you can't prove it in a court of law. A lot of times you learn that the insurance company had to pay the claim even though you know the owner did it. You get frustrated, but inside you know you did the best job you could do. You did your part."

A Final Thought

Accident and fire investigation are specialized areas of forensic science. If you are intrigued by the causes of accidents or fires and are prepared to take on the specific training you'll need, these fields might be the right path for you to take.

4

FORENSIC MEDICINE

"CSI," "BONES," "SECRETS OF THE DEAD"—the number of television shows that center around forensic medicine seems to grow each year. Week after week viewers watch characters perform autopsies and try to identify crime victims. But what does this interesting field really include?

The professional we most readily associate with this area is the forensic pathologist, who utilizes all available information in an attempt to identify an unknown body. For example, the pathologist might make use of medical information about illnesses or operations, matching known scars from a missing person to scars evident on a "found" person.

The team might also include a forensic dentist or odontologist, who will use dental records to help identify a body. And in the case of skeletal remains, the pathologist can call in a forensic anthropologist (see Chapter 5) or an image enhancement specialist to re-create a skull and face.

Some forensic medical teams also include forensic nurses, who work with rape and assault victims and also help in suspicous death investigations.

Forensic Pathology

Pathology is defined as the study of disease or any deviation from a healthy, normal condition. Pathologists examine a body at autopsy and study tissues removed during surgery. They also analyze fluids from the body, such as blood or urine, in the clinical pathology laboratory.

Forensic pathology is a specialization that applies the principles of pathology, and of medicine in general, to the legal needs of society. In other words, forensic pathologists perform autopsies to determine what caused a person's death and how the subject died. Was it a natural death, accidental, suicide, homicide, or undetermined? If the death is found to be criminal, the information the pathologist obtains from the autopsy may be used in a court of law.

Forensic pathologists often go by other job titles, such as *medical examiner, coroner,* or *medicolegal death investigator.* They work mainly with violent deaths, those caused by homicide, accident, or suicide. But they also perform autopsies in other cases, including:

- Sudden death of a seemingly healthy person
- Unattended death (someone who was not under a doctor's care)
- Death while the person is in police custody
- Suspicious or unusual death
- Death from medical malpractice
- Death while in prison

Not all deaths must be reported to the medical examiner or coroner. Local laws determine which deaths must be reported.

Duties

The forensic pathologist's work includes visiting the scene of the death and gathering information about what happened at the time and place of death. The pathologist considers what the person had been doing at the time and assesses the subject's overall health.

During the examination of the body, the forensic pathologist closely studies the person's clothing and the exterior of the body and then conducts an internal exam—the autopsy—concentrating on the organs. The autopsy also may include the study of tissues under a microscope or through the use of x-rays.

The pathologist works in conjunction with other forensic scientists to study the various types of evidence that may be collected. Evidence may include fingernail clippings and scrapings, swabs containing seminal fluid, hair samples, and fibers on the clothing and body, all of which are sent to crime laboratories for examination by a criminalist.

Other specimens obtained at autopsy might be studied by a forensic toxicologist to determine the presence of alcohol, drugs, poisons, or other chemicals. These could be stomach contents, blood, urine, bile, liver, kidney, lungs, brain, fingernail clippings, and hair. Any bullets, shotgun pellets, or wadding recovered at the autopsy are sent to the crime laboratory for examination by a ballistics expert.

During the examination of the body, the pathologist must determine whether injuries were received before or after death occurred and must note any changes that occurred after death, such as the rate of decomposition.

The pathologist must interpret and document patterns of change and injury. He or she must be able to state in a report, and perhaps as an expert witness, that death occurred because of bullet wounds, stab wounds, or blunt force injuries such as those that occur when beaten or when struck by a car. He or she must also determine if the blunt force injuries resulted from an accidental fall. The pattern of injuries also must be examined to rule out or confirm suspected child abuse.

The pathologist coordinates his or her findings with other available information and tries to determine if, for example, the subject died where found or if the body was moved. The time of death is also ascertained.

The forensic pathologist's work must be recorded through a written report and with photographs. The findings may lead to the conviction of a suspect, or it may acquit an innocent person.

Forensic pathologists also work in areas of public health and safety and injury prevention. For example, a pathologist may discover that a child's death was caused by the faulty design of a crib, toy, or article of clothing, or that a vehicle's exhaust system was faulty or the tires were defective. This information can help prevent similar deaths or injuries.

Clinical forensic pathologists work with victims who survived certain injuries or conditions. Because these same injuries or conditions have been witnessed before through autopsies, the pathologist can assist medical doctors in the emergency room, examine wounds, and interpret them for the attending physician and the police.

Training

There's no way around the fact that you will need a lot of training to work as a forensic pathologist. In the first place, you must receive a medical degree, and the formal education and training requirements for physicians are among the most demanding of any occupation: four years of undergraduate school, four years of medical school, and three to eight years of internship and residency, depending on the specialty you select. A few medical schools offer combined undergraduate and medical school programs that last six rather than the customary eight years.

As an undergraduate, your premedical studies will include physics, biology, mathematics, English, and inorganic and organic chemistry, as well as courses in the humanities and social sciences. You may also choose to volunteer at local hospitals or clinics to gain practical experience in the health professions.

The minimum educational requirement for entry into a medical school is three years of college; most applicants, however, have at least a bachelor's degree, and many have advanced degrees. The Association of American Medical Colleges accredits 126 medical schools in the United States and 17 in Canada. These schools either teach allopathic medicine and award a doctor of medicine (M.D.) degree, or they teach osteopathic medicine and award the doctor of osteopathic medicine (D.O.) degree.

Acceptance to medical school is highly competitive. You will be required to submit transcripts, scores from the Medical College Admission Test, and letters of recommendation. In addition, schools will consider your character, personality, leadership qualities, and participation in extracurricular activities. Most schools will require an interview with members of the admissions committee.

Once accepted, you will spend most of the first two years of medical school in laboratories and classrooms taking courses such as anatomy, biochemistry, physiology, pharmacology, psychology, microbiology, pathology, medical ethics, and laws governing medicine. You will also learn to take medical histories, examine patients, and diagnose illnesses. During the last two years, you will work with patients under the supervision of experienced physicians in hospitals and clinics, learning acute, chronic, preventive, and rehabilitative care. You will gain experience in the diagnosis and treatment of illness through rotations in internal medicine, family practice, obstetrics and gynecology, pediatrics, psychiatry, and surgery.

Following medical school, almost all M.D.s enter a residency. At this stage of training, you will pursue graduate medical education in a specialty that takes the form of paid on-the-job training, usually in a hospital. Most D.O.s serve a twelve-month rotating internship after graduation and before entering a residency, which may last two to six years. All states and provinces license physicians. To be licensed, you must graduate from an accredited medical school, pass a licensing examination, and complete one to seven years of graduate medical education.

A physician's training is expensive, and although education costs have increased, student financial assistance has not. Over 80 percent of medical students borrow money to cover their expenses. The high salaries doctors often command are offset the first few years in practice by the need to pay back hefty student loans.

Specializations

M.D.s and D.O.s seeking board certification in a specialty may spend up to seven years in residency training, depending on the specialty. A final examination immediately after residency or after one or two years of practice also is necessary for certification by a member board of the American Board of Medical Specialists (ABMS) or the American Osteopathic Association (AOA). The ABMS represents twenty-four specialty boards, ranging from allergy and immunology to urology. The AOA has approved eighteen specialty boards, ranging from anesthesiology to surgery. For certification in a subspecialty, physicians usually need another one to two years of residency.

To learn more about specific requirements, visit the American Board of Pathology website at www.abpath.org, or the Canadian Association of Pathologists at www.cap.med.org.

Salaries

Physicians have among the highest earnings of any occupation. According to the American Medical Association, the average annual income for pathologists after expenses is $200,000. Income will vary widely according to number of years in practice, geographic region, hours worked, and skill, personality, and professional reputation. The sample jobs listed in this chapter include salary ranges.

Forensic Dentistry and Odontology

Forensic odontology, also referred to as *forensic dentistry*, is part of forensic medicine and the general field of the forensic sciences. The services of forensic dentists are required in four areas:

1. Identification of deceased people through dental remains
2. Bite mark analysis; determining or ruling out possible suspects in crimes in which bite marks are left on a victim or other object
3. Examination of oral-facial structures for determining patient/doctor disputes such as possible malpractice or to prove or disprove insurance fraud
4. Age estimation through dental features

Most of a forensic dentist's workload revolves around the identification of deceased people. A forensic dentist is asked to help identify unknown victims of accidents, homicides, or mass disasters such as floods, earthquakes, or airline crashes.

Identification of humans by means of teeth, dental work, and other oral characteristics has been used for centuries. Here are some fascinating examples:

- In 1066 in England, a story circulated that William the Conqueror, known to have an unusual malocclusion, made the official seal of England by biting into the wax.
- In 1477 in France, the cadaver of Charles, Duke of Burgundy, was identified by the absence of some anterior teeth.
- In 1776 in Massachusetts, General Joseph Warren's body was exhumed and identified by a piece of walrus tusk that had replaced a canine tooth.
- In 1850 in the United States, John White Webster was the first person convicted of murder based on dental evidence.
- In 1925 in the United States, a chemist attempted to defraud his insurance company by setting fire to his lab and leaving an unrecognizable charred corpse behind. Although his wife identified it as the chemist by his two missing teeth, closer examination revealed that the teeth had only recently been removed—the cavities were not fully healed. The chemist had lost his two teeth years before.
- In 1948 in England, the Gorringe case was the first murder to be solved using bite-mark evidence.
- In 1976 in the United States, computers were first used for dental identification in a mass disaster: 139 victims of the Big Thompson Canyon Flood.

• In 1979 in the United States, bite-mark evidence was used in convicting serial killer Ted Bundy.

• In 1979 near Chicago, American Airlines Flight 191 crashed and 274 people lost their lives. Dental identification was performed by two teams of ten dentists.

• In 1979 in Guyana, computers helped with the dental identification of 913 victims of a mass cult suicide/murder led by James Jones in the People's Temple at Jonestown.

• In 1979, California became the first state to implement a statewide dental identification program to process dental records submitted by law enforcement agencies and coroners throughout California and other states.

Forensic odontological identification is based on comparing dental records made during the victim's lifetime with data collected after death. The antemortem data are usually found in dental records, which consist of x-rays, charts, impressions, and study models of the teeth, jaws, and dentures.

A forensic dentist also may be called as an expert witness to give testimony concerning scientific investigation or to provide professional opinions about evidence introduced into a trial.

Training

To work as a forensic odontologist, you must have special knowledge in certain areas, such as familiarity with the unique characteristics of the teeth and the resistance of teeth and tooth restorations under different kinds of environmental stresses. You will also need to adhere to the special laws and regulations that govern professional activities. The prerequisites for this field include an educational background in dentistry, preferably a doctoral degree, in addition to a D.D.S. or D.M.D.

However, the forensic dental team includes professionals other than dentists, such as dental hygienists and assistants. Those members of the team who are not licensed dentists are supervised by the team leader, a professional forensic odontologist.

A dental education will provide you with the fundamentals required for the tasks encountered during forensic work. The skills you will need include the ability to recognize:

- Each tooth in and out of the mouth
- Different tooth surfaces
- Types of filling materials
- Racial and sociological differences in dentition
- Characteristics of oral pathology and close-up photography

In addition, you should also pursue specialized postgraduate training in the field of forensic dentistry. There are currently several courses offered in the United States and Canada; many teach the fundamentals of evidence collection and handling, charting systems, and autopsy protocol. You can locate a program by searching the accredited dental schools listed by the American Dental Association at www.ada.org and the Canadian Dental Association at www.cda-adc.ca.

You must be licensed to practice dentistry in all states and provinces. To qualify for licensure, you must graduate from a dental school that is accredited by the American Dental Association's Commission on Dental Accreditation or the National Dental

Examining Board of Canada. You must also pass written and practical examinations.

Although all dental schools require a minimum of two years of college-level predental education, most dental students have at least a bachelor's degree. Your predental studies will include courses in science, and many applicants to dental school major in a science such as biology or chemistry, while others major in another subject and take many science courses as well. A few applicants are accepted to dental school after two or three years of college and complete their bachelor's degree while attending dental school.

All dental schools in the United States require applicants to take the Dental Admissions Test (DAT); students in Canada must take the Dental Aptitude Test (DAT). Schools will consider your DAT score, grade point average, and information gathered through recommendations and interviews. Competition for admission is keen.

Dental school usually lasts four academic years. Your studies will begin with classroom instruction and laboratory work in basic sciences, including anatomy, microbiology, biochemistry, and physiology. You will also take classes in clinical sciences, including laboratory techniques. During the last two years, you will begin to treat patients, usually in dental clinics, under the supervision of licensed dentists. Most dental schools award the degree of doctor of dental surgery (D.D.S.); the rest award an equivalent degree, doctor of dental medicine (D.M.D.).

The American Board of Forensic Odontology (ABFO) offers certification to qualified candidates in the United States and Canada. You must pass a comprehensive written and oral examination to complete certification. To view the guidelines and application procedure, visit www.abfo.org.

Training for Dental Assistants

The forensic odontology team also includes dental assistants who work under the supervision of the licensed dentist. Because an assistant must be a second pair of hands for a dentist, you must be reliable, work well with others, and have good manual dexterity. Most assistants learn their skills on the job, but you may also choose accredited dental-assisting programs offered by community and junior colleges, trade schools, technical institutes, or the armed forces.

Programs include classroom, laboratory, and preclinical instruction in dental-assisting skills and related theory, as well as practical experience in dental schools, clinics, or dental offices. Most programs take one year or less to complete and lead to a certificate or diploma. Two-year programs offered in community and junior colleges lead to an associate degree.

Most states and provinces regulate the duties that dental assistants are allowed to perform through licensure or registration, which may require passing a written or practical examination. Since the requirements vary by locality, you should check with your state or province to determine its policies. In addition, individual states and provinces have adopted different standards for dental assistants who perform certain advanced duties, such as radiological procedures.

Training for Dental Hygienists

To work as a dental hygienist you must be licensed by the state or province in which you practice. In most localities, you must graduate from an accredited dental hygiene school and pass both a written and clinical examination. Licensure is governed by the American Dental Association's Joint Commission on National Dental Examinations (www.ada.org/prof/prac/licensure) and Canada's National Dental Hygiene Certification Board (www.ndhcb.ca).

Requirements vary from one school to another. Schools offer laboratory, clinical, and classroom instruction in subjects such as anatomy, physiology, chemistry, microbiology, pharmacology, nutrition, radiography, histology (the study of tissue structure), periodontology (the study of gum diseases), pathology, dental materials, clinical dental hygiene, and social and behavioral sciences.

Most dental hygiene programs grant an associate degree, although some also offer a certificate, a bachelor's degree, or a master's degree. You will generally need at least an associate degree or certificate in dental hygiene for practice in a private dental office. A bachelor's or master's degree usually is required for research, teaching, or clinical practice in public or school health programs.

Work Settings

Work settings include employment at a dental school or on an individual contract basis with a law enforcement agency. For those working at a dental school, the opportunity exists to teach forensic dentistry and to conduct research projects, in addition to involvement in actual casework.

Most forensic dentists today work in private practice, however. They are usually associated with the law enforcement agencies of the county in which they live or work, and they provide forensic services on a contractual basis.

The work is sporadic and unpredictable. A forensic dental consultant never knows when he or she will be called upon to help. As a result, most have other work that provides a primary income, such as a dental practice or a teaching position.

Salaries

Salaries for dentists vary according to experience, location, and specialty. For example, self-employed dentists in private practice generally earn more than salaried dentists.

According to the U.S. Bureau of Labor Statistics, salaried dentists have median annual earnings of $129,920. Statistics Canada reports median earnings of $96,443. Median hourly earnings of dental hygienists in the United States are $28.05. Dental hygienists in Canada have median hourly earnings of $33.29. Dental assistants in the United States have median hourly earnings of $13.62; median earnings for those in Canada are $18.66.

Benefits vary substantially by practice setting and may be contingent upon full-time employment. Almost all full-time dental hygienists and assistants employed by private practitioners receive paid vacation time.

Dental assistants working on a forensics team would be paid either by the hour or as a part of the contract fee-for-service arrangement.

Forensic Nursing

The rapidly growing specialty of forensic nursing is defined as the application of nursing science or skills to legal proceedings. Practitioners are registered nurses with additional training who work with scientific and legal investigations and treatment of trauma and/or death of victims of abuse, violence, criminal activity, and traumatic accidents.

Forensic nurses work directly with individual patients, including victims and perpetrators. In addition to providing care, they perform legal duties such as taking specimens from individuals for a rape kit.

They provide consultation to other nursing or medical departments and to law enforcement agencies. And, like most forensics experts, they provide court testimony in areas dealing with trauma, evidence collection, preservation, and analysis; and/or questioned-death investigative processes.

In addition to the areas mentioned above, forensic nurses also make a significant contribution in forensic psychiatric practice and in the treatment of incarcerated patients. (See Chapter 6.)

The International Association of Forensic Nurses (IAFN) provides information on this exciting field. Currently, IAFN is the only membership organization directly serving the educational and professional needs of forensic nurses everywhere. Visit www.iafn.org for information.

Training

It is difficult to find a bachelor's-level program that leads to a degree in forensic nursing in North America. The best route is to pursue a B.S.N. in nursing and then take additional course work or go on for a master's degree in forensic nursing. The IAFN website lists graduate programs in both the United States and Canada. Go to www.iafn.org.

In all states and provinces, you must graduate from a nursing program and pass a national licensing examination to obtain a nursing license. Licenses must be periodically renewed, and some jurisdictions require continuing education for renewal.

There are three major educational paths to nursing that you can pursue:

- Associate degree in nursing (A.D.N.)
- Bachelor of science degree in nursing (B.S.N.)
- Nursing diploma

Associate degree in nursing programs, offered by community and junior colleges, take about two years to complete. About half of all R.N. programs are at the A.D.N. level.

Bachelor of science degree in nursing programs, offered by colleges and universities, take four or five years to complete. About one-fourth of all programs offer degrees at the bachelor's level.

Diploma programs, given in hospitals, last two to three years. Only a small number of programs, about 4 percent, offer diploma-level degrees. Generally, licensed graduates of any of the three program types qualify for entry-level positions as staff nurses.

All nursing education programs include classroom instruction and supervised clinical experience in hospitals and other health care facilities. You will take courses in anatomy, physiology, microbiology, chemistry, nutrition, psychology and other behavioral sciences, and nursing. Your course work will also include the liberal arts for the A.D.N. and B.S.N. degrees.

Supervised clinical experience is provided in hospital departments such as pediatrics, psychiatry, maternity, and surgery. A growing number of programs include clinical experience in nursing care facilities, public health departments, home health agencies, and ambulatory clinics.

If you are considering forensic nursing, you should carefully consider taking the B.S.N. route, which will provide broader advancement opportunities. In fact, many career paths are open only to nurses with bachelor's or advanced degrees. A bachelor's degree is usually necessary for administrative positions and is a prerequisite for admission to graduate nursing programs in forensics, research, consulting, teaching, or the different clinical specializations.

Many A.D.N. and diploma-trained nurses enter bachelor's programs to prepare for a broader scope of nursing practice. They often can find a hospital position and then take advantage of tuition reimbursement programs to work toward a B.S.N.

Salaries

The U.S. Bureau of Labor Statistics reports that median annual earnings of registered nurses are $52,330. The majority earn between $43,370 and $63,360. According to Statistics Canada, median earnings for registered nurses with one to four years of experience are $22.94 per hour; those with five to nine years' experience earn $25.91.

Many employers offer flexible work schedules, child care, educational benefits, and bonuses.

Sample Jobs

The following sample job advertisements will give you an idea of the qualifications needed, the responsibilities, and the salary levels that different job titles offer. When you are ready to look for employment, an Internet search should provide you with numerous available positions.

Deputy Medical Examiner

County is seeking applications from qualified candidates for the newly established position of deputy medical examiner. This position will support the chief medical examiner in the professional and managerial operations of the office. He/she will have a special role in the establishment and monitoring of office procedures, as well as being responsible for performing postmortem examinations. The deputy medical examiner position involves a high degree of independent judgment and requires the ability to work in a collaborative manner.

Requirements include a license to practice medicine in the state as an M.D. or D.O. and board-certified or board-eligible in anatomic and forensic pathology by the American Board of Pathology. Salary: up to $160,000.

Forensic Pathologist/Assistant Medical Examiner

Medical examiner's office is seeking applicants for the position of forensic pathologist/assistant medical examiner. Qualifications include being board certified in AP/CP and board certified, or eligible, in FP. Applicant must be a team player and interested in working in a friendly and exciting environment. Interest in education is a plus.

Responsibilities include performing approximately 250 forensic and nonforensic autopsies per year, acting as assistant medical examiner, and providing education and training to students and residents in forensic pathology. Salary: $65,000 to $89,000.

Forensic Pathologist

County forensic science center is seeking applicants for the position of forensic pathologist. Qualifications include graduation from an accredited school of medicine, completion of a residency in anatomic pathology, one year of experience performing medicolegal autopsies, and a valid license to practice medicine. Certification in forensic pathology by the American Board of Pathology will be required at the time of appointment, or within three years, as a condition of employment.

Responsibilities include performing medicolegal autopsies, testifying in court, and taking death scene calls. This is a new appointment created due to an increased caseload of the office per year. Weekend call will be once every fifth weekend. Salary: $93,000 to $100,000.

Forensic Pathologist

A private forensic consultants group is seeking applicants for the position of forensic pathologist. Qualifications include board certification in anatomic, clinical, and forensic pathology and a state license.

Responsibilities include participating in a moderately active sheriff-coroner autopsy service in two counties. This position will join three forensic pathologists in a private group who serve the public sector. Salary: $120,000 to $150,000.

Senior Histologist

County medical examiner's office is seeking applicants for the position of senior histologist. Qualifications include a high school diploma or G.E.D. Must be a graduate of a National Accredited Agency of Clinical Laboratory Scientist (NAACLS)–accredited histotechnology program or have histology certification by the American Society of Clinical Pathologists, and must have a minimum of two years of full-time work experience in a histology laboratory. Practical knowledge of operation and maintenance of microtome, automatic stainer, automatic slide, coverslipper, and tissue processor is desired, as well as knowledge of laboratory safety rules, regulations, and procedures.

Responsibilities include procuring, preparing, and staining tissue sections to assist the pathologist in making microscopic diagnoses; allocating casework to the histology technician of the section depending on relative abilities and experiences; monitoring analytical standards to ensure that consistency and high quality are maintained at all times; maintaining safe and orderly work areas according to the medical examiner's policies, methods manual, safety and QA/QC procedures; participating in the training and competency testing of new analysts and interns according to sectional protocols; responding to proficiency testing requirements and following all protocols; and assisting the laboratory director as needed.

The person in this position will be exposed to microbiological infections present in case samples, normal laboratory chemicals, and instruments. Some heavy lifting is required. Employment is contingent upon passing a criminal background check. Salary: $22,992 to $39,000.

Forensic Dentist

Forensic dentist needed to join team of medical experts. Must be board certified and actively practicing. This is a physician-managed professional organization whose purpose is to assist attorneys in the evaluation of potential medical malpractice, personal injury, toxic tort, and product liability cases.

Position is responsible for reviewing documented material (medical records, depositions, etc.) and then rendering a nonbiased, objective opinion about the merits (or lack of merit) of the case. If supportable, dentist will then agree to be available for review of additional records, telephone conferences, and testimony in depositions and trial appearances until the case is concluded. The annual caseload per specialist will vary. Consultation is provided on a fixed hourly fee basis.

Firsthand Account

A forensic nurse has shared her personal account; read on to find out what this work is really like.

Patricia Speck, Forensic Nurse

Patricia Speck graduated from the University of Tennessee Health Science Center, College of Nursing, with her bachelor of science and master of science in nursing. In 2005 she earned the doctor in nursing science in public health nursing with a forensic nursing emphasis from the same institution and joined its faculty in 2006. She holds national certification as a family nurse practitioner and is a fellow in the American Academy of Nursing and a distinguished fellow in the International Association of Forensic Nurses.

She shares here her experiences as coordinator of the forensic nursing activity for the City of Memphis, Division of Public Services and Neighborhoods, Sexual Assault Resource Center (SARC).

Getting Started

In 1983 Patricia needed a research topic for her thesis and found it in the Rape Crisis Center (RCC) with a group of nurses who evaluated victims and collected evidence in a community-based clinic. She was attracted to the center because it suited her need for an independent nursing role that utilized her nurse practitioner skills.

While she was completing her graduate thesis and employed full-time as a family nurse practitioner at the county health department, she also volunteered at the RCC and implemented her graduate research. She was then hired as a nurse clinician to see patients on a part-time basis and to train the other staff in the care of the pediatric victim (her expertise was pediatrics).

After she had spent several years volunteering and conducting research at the agency, developing policies and procedures, making recommendations to the non-nursing management, and being on-call with the pool of part-time nurses, the manager of the agency asked her to write the job description for the nursing coordinator.

The medical director of the RCC encouraged her to take the job. She agreed but realized that the position would be solitary and without parallel, so she also kept her public health position as a nurse practitioner. Five years later she left the public health position to work exclusively at the RCC.

What the Work Is Like

Patricia coordinates the registered forensic nurses employed by the City of Memphis Sexual Assault Resource Center (SARC). The nurses are all advanced practice R.N.s who have additional training in the identification and management of victims and offenders of interpersonal violence (IPV).

As a supervisor, she is on call around the clock. Although that may seem demanding, in reality she receives few calls from the police or the newer nurses.

In a typical day she might field a call from the police dispatch wanting to assemble the sexual assault response team (SART) because there's been an assault reported. The SART is a response team made up of a forensic nurse, a member of the law enforcement agency, and a patient advocate who join together to create a multidisciplinary approach to the plight of the rape victim. The R.N. is the only licensed professional in the group. The police are the investigators who must determine if a crime has been committed. The advocate is the bridge between the health care response and the criminal justice system. In Patricia's agency, advocates are now called *law enforcement liaisons.*

She explains that although law enforcement may initiate the team, any member can initiate the response. For instance, if a victim goes to the clinic rather than to the police, the clinic staff assembles the team. If the victim does not want to report a crime, the team is not assembled because the case will not move forward in the criminal justice system, and there is no need for law enforcement or advocacy. The nurse examiner will provide therapeutic care and follow-up instructions to the patient and will refer her to the appropriate mental health and medical providers.

Depending on the situation, Patricia might talk to the patient and then talk to district attorneys about evidence and court testimony in that or other upcoming trials.

She also hires and trains new nurses and students and works with patients' lab results. She discusses cases with the nurses and briefs them after dealing with an assault case. Debriefing is the process of defining an event, and she debriefs students and staff to prevent burnout and help model appropriate internalization of the event.

On any given day, Patricia's responsibilities may include working on policies, procedures, schedules, or payroll. One morning each week she attends a staff meeting where the previous week's cases are reviewed.

If a nurse is unable to cover a shift and Patricia cannot find a replacement, she fills the shift herself, if possible. Another part of her job is professional training and consultation, and she teaches physicians, nurses, attorneys, and judges about the forensic nurse's role and competency. She has also had the opportunity to provide education through the Department of Health for beginning nurse examiners in the state.

Patricia is also responsible for coordinating forensic and nursing education for Memphis Sexual Assault Resource Center (MSARC) forensic nurses, which usually takes place during bimonthly staff meetings. She also serves on citywide committees, acts as the Occupational Safety and Health Administration educator for the agency, and provides periodic tuberculosis screening for the staff.

Sample Cases

Patricia recalls two particular cases. In one, a table dancer was lured to a vehicle in the parking lot of her place of employment early one morning, where she was beaten and raped by three unknown males. When she was released, she called law enforcement to report the crime. Police paged the forensic nurse, who met them at the clinic after calling the patient advocate. The nurse provided support and crisis intervention, physically evaluated the victim's injuries, made recommendations for referral, collected evidence (physical and verbal), and treated the victim with medications to prevent infection and pregnancy.

The forensic nurse transferred the information to law enforcement professionals and placed the evidence into a secured location, waiting for transport by law enforcement.

The fact that the victim was a table dancer might have adversely affected the prosecution of this case, but the photographic documentation persuaded the prosecutor to move forward. However, because there were no visible injuries to the face and head, the charges were reduced to simple assault, and the offenders pleaded guilty and served no jail time.

In another case, a grandmother was undressing her four-year-old granddaughter for a bath and discovered bruises around both the child's nipples. The grandmother was distressed because another child in her family had died from a cancer whose first symptoms were bruising on the chest, so she took the child to the local emergency department.

The physician in the emergency department recognized the patterned injury as bite marks and called the police, who paged the forensic nurse to come to the hospital.

The nurse paged the advocate, and they arrived at the hospital with law enforcement. The nurse collaborated with the physician before and during the evaluation and then provided support and crisis intervention, physically evaluated the child from head to toe, collected evidence (physical and verbal), and made recommendations for referral and follow-up to the grandmother and the physician. The evidence was transported to a secured location awaiting transport by law enforcement officials.

The patient's grandmother called the next day to report that the child had disclosed who had bitten her, and the police arrested the offender.

Another forensic nurse was called to draw the suspect's blood for DNA analysis. In this case, Patricia did not have to testify because DNA evidence from the saliva left on the breast matched the DNA of the offender, and the offender pleaded guilty.

Upsides and Downsides

Patricia describes herself as an adrenaline junkie who thrives in busy environments. For this reason, working in the RCC suits her very well. It is never boring, but she finds that the work sometimes can be emotionally traumatic—for instance, the discovery of a permanent, incurable, sexually transmitted disease in a child or facilitating in the removal of a teenager from his or her home. On the other hand, the patient population is generally very needy, and interventions provide opportunities for patients to thrive in spite of their traumas. Another rewarding part of the job is training and empowering new nurses who are entering the field.

She finds that the most challenging part of her job is maintaining an open and accepting mind about patients and providers and accepting that the patient may have seedy and secret activities and criminal motives that supersede victim status. It is also challenging to keep an open mind with other professionals who verbalize their bias either for or against the victim.

Finally, Patricia dislikes non-nursing professionals who step into her practice without the proper education or licensure and tell her what should be done during the nursing evaluation and intervention with the patient.

Advice from a Professional

Patricia recommends attending a nursing school where there is a forensic nursing center to visit and observe. To become a leader in the field, go to an accredited school of nursing that supports forensic nursing education at all levels, from undergraduate to doctoral studies.

Specifically, she says, "For credibility in court, add nurse practitioner education and experience on the way. To create a comprehensive educational experience, get the forensic studies for credit while matriculating through family, community, maternal child, or psych/mental health nursing programs."

A Final Thought

The field of forensic medicine is clearly for those with a predisposition toward medical or dental studies. If your interests lie in these demanding areas, you might want to expand your options by focusing on forensics as a career choice.

5

FORENSIC ANTHROPOLOGY

THE AMERICAN BOARD of Forensic Anthropology defines this profession as the application of the science of physical anthropology to the legal process. The identification of skeletal, badly decomposed, or otherwise unidentified human remains is important for both legal and humanitarian reasons—forensic anthropologists apply standard scientific techniques developed in physical anthropology to identify such remains and to assist in the detection of crime.

Randy Skelton, anthropologist at the University of Montana, Missoula, explains: "Methods and techniques to assess age, sex, stature, ancestry, and analyze trauma and disease are generally developed to help anthropologists understand different populations living all over the world at different times throughout history. When we take these methods and apply them to unknown modern human remains, with the aim of establishing identity or manner of death, then we are practicing the forensic application of osteology."

Forensic anthropologists frequently work in conjunction with forensic pathologists, odontologists, and homicide investigators to identify a corpse, discover evidence of foul play, and/or establish the postmortem interval. In addition to assisting in locating and recovering suspicious remains, forensic anthropologists work to suggest the age, sex, ancestry, stature, and unique features of a decedent from the skeleton.

In recent years, forensic anthropologists have also begun to work on identifying the remains of victims of homicides, mass disasters, and political atrocities.

Forensic anthropologists also apply their skills to other issues. For example, Dr. Douglas Ubekaler, forensic anthropologist at the Smithsonian Institution, examines the problems of the homeless in contemporary society. "By looking at the pattern of trauma and disease on the skeleton, we could learn a lot about his lifestyle, which in turn tells us something about the biology of the homeless."

Branches of Anthropology

There are three major subfields or branches of anthropology: cultural, archaeological, and physical. Linguistics is sometimes included as a fourth subfield.

Cultural anthropology deals with the different aspects of human society, culture, behavior, beliefs, ways of life, and so on. It can include the study of both nontechnologic societies and technologic societies, past and present.

Archaeology is the study of past cultures through artifacts and the material remains of people. The lifestyles of past peoples may be studied from what they leave behind, which can range from small shards of pottery to large dwellings such as huts or houses of worship. Archaeological research covers a vast array of cultures, from prehistory to our recent past, all over the world.

The archaeological methods used in uncovering artifacts are very useful to forensic anthropologists. Other disciplines that can overlap with archaeology include geology, geography, ecology, and history.

Physical—also known as biological—anthropology deals with the physical and biological aspects of the primate order: humans, chimps, gorillas, monkeys, and so on, both past and present. Some of the specialized areas covered under this largest subfield of anthropology include the following:

- Primatology—primate biology and behavior
- Osteology—study of bones
- Paleoanthropology—study of primate evolution
- Paleodemography—vital statistics of past populations
- Skeletal biology
- Human variation and adaptation
- Genetics
- Nutrition
- Dental anthropology

Most forensic anthropologists are primarily trained in physical anthropology. Forensic anthropology is an applied area, borrowing methods and techniques developed from skeletal biology and osteology and applying them to forensic cases.

Some forensic anthropologists are skilled in the art of facial reproduction, which involves the modeling of how a face may have appeared in the living subject using the only surviving evidence—a skull. Artists and sculptors also work in this area.

Other forensic anthropologists are experts in determining the length of time elapsed since death by examining insect remains and states of body decomposition.

With their naturalistic approach to recovery of skeletons, examination of animal remains, and analysis of soil and vegetation patterns, forensic anthropologists can successfully recover human remains from different kinds of terrain, such as deserts or forests.

Training

Although there are no actual programs in forensic anthropology, you can major in anthropology at the undergraduate level and then go on for a master's, or preferably a Ph.D., specializing in physical anthropology or anatomy.

If you want to pursue forensic anthropology, one of the best courses of action is to seek out a mentor, take additional courses and workshops in related forensic sciences, and participate in internships in appropriate settings, such as in a medical examiner's office.

Because most forensic anthropologists work in universities, a Ph.D. is almost always the basic requirement. Forensic anthropologist Dr. A. Midori Albert, who provides a firsthand account at the end of this chapter, offers the following advice: "The best way to approach your education in forensic anthropology is to realize that, above all, you are an anthropologist first . . . your specialty in the applied area of forensic science is secondary."

Dr. Albert advises that you do not have to specialize during your undergraduate studies. You will most likely be required to take classes in each of the three subfields of anthropology, focusing on the following:

- **Cultural anthropology.** Behaviors, rituals, belief systems, economies, kinship, traditions, history, language, art, and so forth, of various societies throughout the world, past and present
- **Archaeology.** Reconstructing the lives of ancient or historic peoples from their material remains (artifacts), or studying what modern people leave behind
- **Physical/biological anthropology.** Aspects of human beings—bones, diet and nutrition, growth, disease, reproduction, adaptation, human evolution; aspects of primates—behaviors, evolution, and ecology

Your program may also include studies in linguistics, which is the study of languages and their origins.

Dr. Albert recommends using your undergraduate studies to familiarize yourself with the different areas of anthropology, gaining a solid foundation from which you can branch out into a specialization. For example, if you focus on physical anthropology, you can specialize in osteology, which can later be applied to forensic settings.

You should also take courses in genetics, biology, chemistry, physics, anatomy/physiology, zoology, and statistics. Many of these classes also will satisfy your basic studies or core freshman and sophomore requirements.

"To be admitted to graduate school in anthropology, you should have a bachelor's degree in anthropology, or at the very least a minor or its equivalent," says Dr. Albert. "By equivalent I mean at least one anthropology survey course in each of the subfields: cultural, archaeology, physical, and language and culture or linguistics, if offered. Statistics would be great and is highly recommended. A history and theory class in anthropology would further enhance your minor, if it's not already required. Any undergraduate courses in anatomy/physiology or vertebrate anatomy also would be a tremendous benefit. I highly recommend genetics."

She also stresses the importance of earning a high grade point average and high score on the Graduate Record Examination. Take prep classes, read books, use CDs and DVDs designed to help you study—do whatever you can to enhance your scores.

Any undergraduate research you can do will also be a great help. Dr. Albert suggests getting to know your professors, finding out what research they're involved in and making time to volunteer. Good recommendation letters from professors who know you will be vital to your success. You must also develop strong writing skills to help you prepare the best possible application essay and to help in your studies and your career.

In searching for an M.A. program, Dr. Albert says, "Don't worry about going into a program where there is no forensic anthropologist on the faculty. Find an excellent osteologist or skeletal biologist with whom to study, to be your mentor. What you need at this level is a solid background in physical anthropology and, more important, osteology. Become proficient with statistics. Learn to identify bones, how to analyze them, what interpretations and explanations can be made from those analyses—in every context, not just the forensic context. The forensic applications can be learned later, at the Ph.D. level or even beyond. And, after a good foundation at the M.A. level, it will be all the more easy to understand the forensic applications of bone analyses."

Most students finish the M.A. in anthropology in two to three years. The time to complete a Ph.D. varies widely and may take five to eight years or more. It also takes time to gain experience teaching, which is important if you plan to teach at the college level.

"In summary," Dr. Albert says, "it may take as few as five years or up to eight or ten years to get your M.A. and Ph.D. in anthropology, if you're going to specialize in osteology or skeletal biology. You may learn the forensic applications along the way, or you may choose to learn them at the postdoctorate level. It is important not to rush. What good are the degrees if you're not well trained, not confident in what you know, and have no jobs to apply for? Timing is more important than time."

Job Settings

Unfortunately, forensic anthropology offers few opportunities for full-time employment. Virtually all the forensic anthropologists in the United States and Canada have Ph.D.s in anatomy or physical anthropology; with very few exceptions, they hold academic positions in departments of anthropology or archaeology and practice forensic anthropology as a sideline.

Most of those working outside the university environment are employed by medical examiner's offices or law-enforcement agencies, work as curators in museums, or work in local, state, or federal crime labs as regular staff members who happen to have expertise in forensic anthropology.

Some work for the armed forces, and some are self-employed, offering their services nationally to federal agencies or to any local law-enforcement agency that doesn't have a nearby forensic anthropologist to rely on.

Finding a Job

The American Anthropological Association (AAA) operates a placement service designed to aid anthropologists in their search for jobs and to facilitate communication between job seekers and employers. At the annual meeting, the placement service is open free of charge to all association members; it provides job boards that list available jobs, a message center for communication between job seekers and employers, and interview space.

You may search for available jobs in the United States and Canada at the association's website, where you will also find complete information about how to utilize the job placement service. Visit www.aaanet.org for details.

Other outlets for job hunting are the usual networking, classified ads in local papers for law enforcement agencies, and in the *Chronicle of Higher Education* for academic placement.

Salaries

Salaries in forensic anthropology vary widely, depending on your level of education and experience, work setting, and geographic location. Dr. Albert reveals that she earns more than $45,000 a year for a nine-month contract. The actual amount varies based on the activities that generate additional income, such as online courses, workshops, and consulting.

According to the U.S. Bureau of Labor Statistics, anthropologists in general have median annual earnings of about $44,000. In the federal government, anthropologists with a bachelor's degree and no experience could start at a yearly salary between $25,000 and $31,000, depending on their college records. Those with a master's degree could start at $37,400, and those with a Ph.D. degree could begin at $45,240. Some individuals with experience and an advanced degree could start at $54,222.

Sample Job

The following sample job advertisement will give you an idea of the qualifications needed and the responsibilities necessary for a job in forensic anthropology. When you are ready to look for employment, an Internet search should provide you with numerous available positions.

Full-time Faculty Position

> The University Department of Sociology, Anthropology, and Criminology invites applications for a full-time, tenure-track faculty position at the assistant level. The position offers the opportunity to teach law and other graduate students. Qualifications include a Ph.D. in sociology, anthropology, criminology, or criminal justice; teaching expertise in the area of legal anthropology and in one or more of the following areas: juvenile delinquency, gender, family, victimology, comparative criminal justice, violent crime, and/or organized crime. Proven record of research and publication in these or related fields and a commitment to teaching excellence are required.

Firsthand Account

Read the following account of an experienced professional in this fascinating field to see if this might be the career for you.

Dr. A. Midori Albert, Forensic Anthropologist

A. Midori Albert is an assistant professor in the anthropology department at the University of North Carolina at Wilmington. In her role as forensic anthropologist, she also works as a consultant with the military and local law-enforcement agencies.

Dr. Albert earned her B.A. in psychology with a minor in anthropology from the University of Florida in Gainesville. That was followed by an M.A. in anthropology from the University of Florida and a Ph.D. in anthropology from the University of Colorado at Boulder. She accomplished all this within just five years.

She began studying forensic anthropology as a graduate student in 1991 and started working at the University of North Carolina in 1995. She has attended many workshops in forensic sciences, including the International Forensic Photography Workshop, given through the Dade County Medical Examiner Department in Miami, Florida, and the Medicolegal Death Investigators' Training Course in St. Louis, Missouri.

Getting Started

"I was fascinated by the human skeleton and human variation in general, across time and space," Dr. Albert says. "The idea that we could learn about diet, nutrition, trauma, how a person lived and died, was absolutely amazing to me. When I discovered that one could examine unknown contemporary skeletons to assist in establishing identity and manner of death, I knew that was what I wanted to do."

She also liked the academic environment, where she could discover and learn new things, as well as the detective work and the puzzle-solving aspect of the forensic sciences. She says, "To be a professor where I can teach, conduct research, and offer consultations on forensic cases is so rewarding because I get to do the many different things I like."

What the Work Is Like

Dr. Albert explains that forensic anthropology is the application of methods and theories derived from the specializations of human osteology (skeletal biology within the subfield of anthropology known as physical or biological anthropology) and some archaeology, another subfield of anthropology.

Forensic anthropologists draw on skeletal data, formulae, and gross observations to establish an identity profile—to determine sex, age, ancestry, stature—and assess pathology (trauma and/or disease), as well as determine how long a body has been dead. Essentially, forensic anthropologists assist in the identification of people from their skeletal remains and help assess the manner of death.

While a typical day is hard to describe because of her various duties, Dr. Albert lists some of the activities she engages in throughout the semester, which may occur in any combination.

• Teaching courses in general physical anthropology, human osteology, forensic anthropology, primate biology and behavior, dental anthropology, and direct independent study projects
• Attending departmental and university committee meetings (the business end of academia)
• Working in her laboratory, collecting skeletal data, running statistical tests, and analyzing results
• Writing journal articles, since much of forensic anthropology is about research and providing the very data we all rely on when consulting on cases
• Consulting on a forensic case

The consulting work is usually not planned but occurs whenever she receives a call or e-mail about a set of unknown bones that has been discovered. Although most forensic anthropologists work with medical examiners, the chief medical examiner of North Carolina prefers to conduct his own osteological analyses, so most of Dr. Albert's consulting work is with the military, at the Camp LeJeune army base and for the Naval Criminal Investigative Services.

She has also assisted local law enforcement (sheriffs and city police) in the identification of human vs. nonhuman remains. She has searched wooded areas for human remains and has been present for the draining of a pond in search of human remains.

Other consulting work has come from questions of family genealogy and the mystery of unmarked graves. In one such case, Dr. Albert excavated a grave to help identify a family member, and she has also consulted on how to find clandestine graves.

Not all of her work directly involves dead bodies and hands-on activities, however. She also conducts workshops for law enforcement personnel, teaching the vital skills of proper search and recovery methods. "I find this is a major way forensic anthropologists can contribute to the entire team approach to forensic science," says Dr. Albert. "It truly is a multidisciplinary effort."

She also wants to dispel any misconceptions about forensic anthropology. "I want to convey that it's not like we're some weird lab scientists with bubbling potions and ghosts flying around, working in a dark, dingy, musty basement lab. Rather, my lab has two sunny windows and walls in a happy, soothing color. I find my workday is quite pleasant, really, aside from occasional odors.

"The other thing I've found, not through any objective scientific inquiry, is that most folks in the forensic sciences have wonderful senses of humor. I believe it's because the work can be depressing, and naturally optimistic people balance this out."

Upsides and Downsides

What Dr. Albert likes most about her work is the constant challenge and change presented by new research topics, new students, and new cases. She also appreciates the flexibility in her schedule and the freedom to explore areas that she believes need more research.

What she likes least is the struggle to bring the realization and appreciation of the multidisciplinary approach to the forefront of people's minds. "Sometimes I get tied down with the business end of things, leaving less time to study the bones," she says.

Advice from a Professional

Dr. Albert recommends majoring in anthropology as the starting point for a career. You can explore the *American Anthropological Association Guide to Departments of Anthropology*, which is an annual reference book that lists all the anthropology departments in the United States and Canada.

As stated earlier in this chapter, there are no degrees offered in forensic anthropology. The field of study is anthropology, the focus is the subfield of physical/biological anthropology, and the specialization may be human osteology/skeletal biology with a forensic component. Dr. Albert stresses that the emphasis is on breadth at the undergraduate level. Exposure to cultural anthropology, archaeology, physical anthropology, human evolution, genetics, primates, adaptation and variation, osteology, history and theory, and statistics is of utmost importance.

Investigate where you want to go, and find a human osteologist or skeletal biologist active in research. This will ensure that you get a strong, broad background forming a solid foundation in osteology. From there, you can specialize in the forensic aspects of human osteology. For example, Dr. Albert offers undergraduate research opportunities for majors interested in various osteology projects. She feels that this is a great opportunity to gain experience (which makes graduate research easier), to get an edge in applying to graduate school (because you've been able to demonstrate your abilities and show your serious interest), and to basically have fun.

However, you don't need to work with a forensic anthropologist as an undergraduate or as an M.A. student. Most people begin studying forensic anthropology as graduate students or even after the Ph.D. because of the advanced level of statistics, anatomy, and other areas that are needed.

"There's much to know, and it doesn't all happen overnight," Dr. Albert advises. "Be patient and gather as much information and experience as you can. Intern at a medical examiner facility, if possible. Volunteer to work in osteology labs. Be willing to do volunteer work to gain hands-on experience. Attend an archaeology field school if you can to learn excavation techniques.

"The downside of this career is that there are very few jobs. When I explored this career back in 1990, my professor told me there would be no jobs. I went for it anyway, thinking that if I have a passion for what I do, then I'd be good at it. And if I were good at it, surely I could find some way to make a living. I believe I'm extremely fortunate to be where I am today. But, it's like my Ph.D. professor said, 'The harder you work, the luckier you get.' So, it's not luck as much as it is tenacity, patience, attention to detail, thirst for knowledge, endurance, and risk taking that make someone successful in her or his career."

In summary, Dr. Albert says, "If you love bones, in any context, not just the forensic, and if you truly want to satisfy your intellectual curiosity and keep your mind working in amazing ways, then this field is for you. The education and training process can be long and arduous, but if bones are what you love, then the process is just as enjoyable as the outcome.

"It's my opinion that only people who want to do what they love pursue forensic anthropology or an academic career. We don't do it for the money. The rewards are many and difficult to explain to someone who just wants to make big bucks. The luxury of time to think and interact with colleagues and students and laypeople is wonderful."

A Final Thought

Forensic anthropology is a very specialized area of the forensic sciences. If you are interested in uncovering the secrets of the past as you help to solve crimes and investigate mysteries, this area might provide the challenge you are looking for.

6

FORENSIC PSYCHOLOGY AND PSYCHIATRY

As in other areas of the forensic sciences, it's possible that we have gained most of our exposure to forensic psychologists and psychiatrists from books, films, and television shows. You might be familiar with Dr. Alex Cross, either from reading one of several James Patterson novels or from seeing him portrayed on screen by Morgan Freeman. Along with Alex Cross, we see many other fictional psychologists and psychiatrists take the witness stand and offer expert testimony. They build a case for why a defendant committed a crime and should be acquitted. When working for the prosecution, they testify as to why the defendant should be found guilty as charged.

These forensic professionals have other roles, too. They are called on to evaluate a criminal defendant and assess whether he or she is competent to stand trial. They also might help a judge determine if there should be a change of venue for a trial. They work with witnesses to help restore lost memories; they assist in establishing a jury favorable to whichever side has hired the specialist; and they provide behavioral profiles to help law enforcement agencies track down and arrest criminals.

Forensic specialists also help establish guidelines for fair lineups. Or they help a worker's compensation panel determine if vocational rehabilitation plans are feasible.

Broadly defined, clinical psychology is concerned with the assessment and treatment of persons with mental disorders. Clinical-forensic psychologists are clinical psychologists who specialize in the assessment and/or treatment of persons who are involved in the legal process or legal system.

Forensic psychiatry is a subspecialty of medicine. It includes practice, consultation, and research in the areas in which psychiatry is applied to legal issues.

Legal Issues

Forensic psychology and psychiatry cover a broad range of legal issues. In family and domestic relations laws, issues include juvenile delinquency, child custody and visitation, parental fitness, children's need of supervision, abrogation of parental rights, spousal abuse, child neglect, abandonment of children, and adoption and foster care.

Issues in criminal law include the patient's competence to stand trial, to waive legal representation, to be sentenced, to be executed, and whether or not to consider guilt by reason of mental illness or diminished responsibility, and innocence by reason of mental disease or mental defect.

Civil issues include involuntary psychiatric hospitalization; rights to refuse treatment; informed consent; competence to participate in do-not-resuscitate decisions; capacity to testify; competence to become engaged, married, or divorced; contractual capacity; disability compensation; and medical malpractice confidentiality.

Work Settings

Forensic psychologists and psychiatrists may work in secure forensic units in state forensic hospitals, community mental health centers providing specialized services, court clinics, juvenile treatment centers, jails, prisons, specialized agencies, or in private practice conducting forensic evaluation and treatment relevant to legal decision-making. They may also be involved in activities such as teaching, training, or supervision in a department of psychology, a medical school, a hospital, an interdisciplinary institute, or a clinic. Some professionals conduct research and scholarship in areas such as violence risk assessment, treatment needs and response, and decision-making strategies.

Some psychologists and psychiatrists may receive more extensive training in law and earn a J.D. (Juris Doctor) or M.L.S. (Master of Legal Studies) in addition to their training and degrees in psychology or psychiatry. These professionals involve themselves in areas of law relevant to the behavioral sciences and may work in law schools as well as in other academic, medical, or other applied settings as mentioned earlier.

In addition to teaching law, they also may become involved in research or clinical practice (depending on their specialization) or legal practice as an attorney.

Training for Forensic Psychologists and Psychiatrists

If you plan to work as a forensic psychologist, you will major in psychology or a related behavioral science during the first four years of college. You will then go on for one to two years of training for a master's degree or go straight through for a total of four to six postgraduate years to obtain a Ph.D. in psychology.

Following the Ph.D., you may go on to postdoctoral fellowship training in forensic psychology or do independent study and obtain on-the-job training in forensic psychology. You will then apply to the American Board of Forensic Psychology for certification through examination.

There are a few schools offering a dual J.D./M.A. or J.D./Ph.D. degree that combines legal education with training in psychology studies.

To work as a forensic psychiatrist, you must first become a medical doctor. Earning an M.D. involves twelve years of education including college, medical school, and residency training in psychiatry. Forensic psychiatrists also have additional education and experience in areas relevant for the law.

Some forensic psychiatrists take an additional one or two years of postresidency training in psychiatry and the law. Others follow some independent study and on-the-job training. Psychiatrists who have passed a series of examinations are then certified by the American Board of Forensic Psychiatry (ABFP).

Sample Undergraduate Program

A typical undergraduate program in forensic psychology is designed for students who are interested in the relationship between psychology and the criminal justice system. The program offers training in psychological theory, research methods, and the application of psychological principles to specific areas in the legal system. The major provides an interdisciplinary background appropriate for students who intend to pursue careers in psychology, social work, law enforcement, or other criminal justice professions.

Students can receive practical experience in forensic psychology by enrolling in an internship program, which offers fieldwork placements in such settings as hospitals for emotionally disturbed offenders, prisons, and agencies related to the family court.

Sample Undergraduate Courses

Courses run the gamut from introductory psychology to higher-level courses in anthropology, sociology, government, economics, and the law:

General Psychology
Abnormal Psychology
Experimental Psychology
Psychology and the Law
Principles and Methods of Statistics
Ethics and Law
The Family: Change, Challenges, and Crisis Intervention
Social Psychology
Psychology and Women
Child Psychology
Psychology of Adolescence and the Adolescent Offender
Group Dynamics
Theories of Personality
Psychology of Alcoholism

Therapeutic Intervention in Alcoholism
Introduction to Counseling Psychology
Key Concepts in Psychotherapy
Research Methods
Criminology
Juvenile Delinquency
Drug Use and Abuse in American Society
Social Psychology and the Criminal Justice System
Psychological Foundations of Police Work
Correctional Psychology
Family Conflict and the Family Court
Psychology of Criminal Behavior
Fieldwork in Forensic Psychology
Independent Study
Psychological Analysis of Criminal Behavior
Youth, the Family, and Criminal Justice
Psychology of Oppression
Culture and Personality
Systems of Law
Anthropology and the Abnormal
Techniques in Crisis Intervention
Economic Analysis of Crime
Urban Politics
Problems in Civil Rights and Civil Liberties
Violence and Social Change in America
History of Crime and Punishment in the United States
Criminal Law
Crime and Punishment in Literature
Organized Crime in America

Race and Ethnic Relations
Probation and Parole: Principles and Practices
Social Deviance
Penology

Sample Graduate Program and Courses

The program in law and psychology at Simon Fraser University offers doctoral studies in two areas: the experimental-psychology and law stream, and the clinical-forensic stream.

The clinical-forensic stream prepares students in clinical psychology with research and clinical skills unique to the forensic arena. Due to the overlap of the two areas, students in both streams will take many of the same courses and will develop similar research skills; however, students in the clinical-forensic stream will further develop their clinical training to include forensic training and practice experience.

Required Courses
Seminar in Law and Psychology
Special Topics in Civil Forensic Psychology
Special Topics in Criminal Forensic Psychology
Mental Health Law and Policy

Research and Practicum Components
Research Project in Forensic Psychology
Practicum in Forensic Psychology (This may be met in
either a four-month block placement or the equivalent,
for example, two days per week for nine months.)

Forensic Social Work and Mental Health Counseling

Social workers help people function to the best of their ability in their environment, to deal with their relationships with others, and to solve personal and family problems.

Social workers often see clients who face a life-threatening disease or a social problem, such as inadequate housing, unemployment, lack of job skills, financial distress, serious illness or disability, substance abuse, unwanted pregnancy, or antisocial behavior. They also assist families facing serious domestic conflicts, including child or spousal abuse. Through direct counseling, they help clients identify their concerns, consider effective solutions, and find reliable resources.

Social workers typically counsel clients and arrange for services that can help them. Often they refer clients to specialists in services such as debt counseling, child care or elder care, public assistance, or alcohol or drug rehabilitation, and then they follow up with clients to ensure that the services are helpful and that clients make proper use of them. Social workers may review eligibility requirements, help fill out forms and applications, visit clients on a regular basis, and provide support during crises.

In courts and correctional facilities, social workers evaluate and counsel individuals in the criminal justice system to cope better in society. They provide expert testimony on a number of issues including adoption, child custody and visitation, and substance abuse.

Child or adult protective services social workers investigate reports of abuse and neglect and intervene if necessary. They may initiate legal action to remove children from homes and place them temporarily in an emergency shelter or with a foster family.

Criminal justice social workers make recommendations to courts, prepare pre-sentencing assessments, and provide services to prison inmates and their families. Probation and parole officers provide similar services to those sentenced by a court to probation or parole.

Mental health social workers and counselors provide services for people with mental or emotional problems. Such services include individual and group therapy, outreach, crisis intervention, social rehabilitation, and training in skills of everyday living. They also may help plan for supportive services to ease patients' return to the community.

Health care social workers help patients and their families cope with chronic, acute, or terminal illnesses and handle problems that may stand in the way of recovery or rehabilitation. They may organize support groups for families of patients suffering from cancer, AIDS, Alzheimer's disease, or other illnesses. They also advise family caregivers, counsel patients, and help plan for their needs after discharge by arranging for at-home services—from delivery of meals to oxygen equipment. Some work on interdisciplinary teams that evaluate certain kinds of patients, such as geriatric or organ transplant patients, for example.

Some social workers choose to enter private practice. Most are clinical social workers who provide psychotherapy, usually paid through health insurance. Private practitioners typically have at least a master's degree and a period of supervised work experience. A network of contacts for referrals also is essential.

Mental health counselors generally have less involvement with the criminal justice system than social workers; those working in correctional facilities are the most involved.

In general, counselors assist people with personal, family, educational, mental health, and career decisions and problems. Their duties depend on the individuals they serve and the settings in which they work. Many perform the same or similar functions to that of the social worker.

Counselors work in schools, mental health clinics, substance abuse programs, child welfare agencies, domestic violence shelters, rehabilitation clinics, employment centers, vocational training programs, and, of course, prisons, jails, and other criminal justice-related facilities or programs. They consult and work with parents, teachers, school administrators, school psychologists, school nurses, attorneys, police, and social workers.

Training for Forensic Social Workers and Counselors

You will find that a bachelor's in social work (B.S.W.) degree is the most common minimum requirement to qualify for a job as a social worker. However, majoring in psychology, sociology, and related fields may be sufficient to qualify for some entry-level jobs, especially in small community agencies.

Although you will need at least a bachelor's degree, an advanced degree has become the standard for many positions. You'll need to earn a master's in social work (M.S.W.) for positions in health and mental health settings and for certification for clinical work.

Jobs in public agencies also may require an advanced degree, such as a master's in social service policy or administration. Supervisory, administrative, and staff training positions usually require at least an advanced degree. College and university teaching positions and most research appointments normally require a doctorate in social work (D.S.W. or Ph.D.).

There are literally hundreds of accredited B.S.W. and M.S.W. programs in the United States and Canada, as well as dozens of

Ph.D. programs. A good B.S.W. program will prepare you for direct service positions such as caseworker or group worker through courses in social work practice, social welfare policies, human behavior and the social environment, social research methods, social work values and ethics, dealing with a culturally diverse clientele, promotion of social and economic justice, and populations at risk. Accredited B.S.W. programs require at least four hundred hours of supervised field experience.

A master's degree program will prepare you for work in your chosen field of concentration and continue to develop your skills to perform clinical assessments, to manage large caseloads, and to explore new ways of drawing upon social services to meet the needs of clients.

Master's programs last two years and include nine hundred hours of supervised field instruction or internship. A part-time program may take four years. You don't need a B.S.W. to enter a master's program, but courses in psychology, biology, sociology, economics, political science, history, social anthropology, urban studies, and social work are recommended. In addition, a second language may be very helpful. Most master's programs offer advanced standing for those with a bachelor's degree from an accredited social work program.

You must have formal education to work as a counselor. About six out of ten counselors have master's degrees in fields of study including college student affairs, elementary or secondary school counseling, education, gerontological counseling, marriage and family counseling, substance abuse counseling, rehabilitation counseling, agency or community counseling, clinical mental health counseling, counseling psychology, career counseling, and related fields.

Most graduate-level counselor education programs are in departments of education or psychology. Courses are grouped into eight core areas: human growth and development, social and cultural foundations, helping relationships, group work, career and lifestyle development, appraisal, research and program evaluation, and professional orientation.

In an accredited program, forty-eight to sixty semester hours of graduate study, including a period of supervised clinical experience in counseling, are required for a master's degree.

Certification or licensing requirements for counselors vary by state and province. In some areas credentialing is mandatory; in others, it is voluntary.

Clinical mental health counselors usually have a master's degree in mental health counseling, another area of counseling, or in psychology or social work. Voluntary certification is available through the National Board for Certified Counselors, Inc. Generally, to receive certification as a clinical mental health counselor, a counselor must have a master's degree in counseling, two years of postmaster's experience, a period of supervised clinical experience, a taped sample of clinical work, and a passing grade on a written examination.

Psychiatric Technicians

Psychiatric technicians provide nursing and other basic care to mentally ill, emotionally disturbed, or mentally challenged patients. They also work in a forensic capacity with prisoners. (See the first-hand account at the end of this chapter.)

Psychiatric technicians participate in rehabilitation and treatment programs, help with personal hygiene, and administer oral medications and hypodermic injections following a physician's prescriptions and hospital procedures. They monitor a patient's physical and emotional well-being and report to medical staff.

Most psychiatric technicians are trained through postsecondary vocational training programs.

Salaries

Salaries for forensic psychologists and psychiatrists vary according to the setting and nature of the work. In academic settings, the salary for a beginning assistant professor might be in the $55,000 to $65,000 range. Salaries in medical school settings are typically higher, as they are established in comparison with medical professionals. Psychiatry professors in medical school earn some of their salary by obtaining grants or contracts or through clinical services income.

The U.S. Bureau of Labor Statistics provides these average annual salary figures in the different medical specialties, based on less than two years in the specialty:

Anesthesiology	$260,000
Surgery	$229,000
Obstetrics/Gynecology	$203,000
Psychiatry	$174,000
General Internal Medicine	$142,000
General/Family Practice	$137,000
Pediatrics	$133,000

There are striking differences among the different types of correctional settings. Beginning salaries for psychologists in the federal prison system can be more than $50,000 a year. Salaries are often lower in state correctional facilities or local jails. Some correctional facilities might pay different rates depending on whether the job candidate holds an advanced degree.

The starting salary for a doctoral-level psychologist in a hospital or community clinic setting ranges between $50,000 and $60,000.

Psychologists also are able to establish a part-time practice or consulting business in addition to working with an organization. Part-time private practice allows a psychologist or psychiatrist to earn income at an hourly rate consistent with what others charge in the field and geographic area. Rates can vary a great deal, generally between $100 and $300 an hour, depending on the setting and the geographic location.

Forensic psychologists do not usually provide services to parties involved in legal proceedings on a contingency fee basis. Hourly rates or a flat fee is offered for expert testimony and other related services. Some forensic psychologists and psychiatrists, especially those who earn most of their income from forensic work, offer occasional pro bono or reduced rate services.

The average annual salary for psychologists in local government is about $59,000; those working in federal government earn about $66,000. Median annual earnings of social workers in different areas are as follows: child, family, and school social workers, $37,480; medical and public health social workers, $43,040; and mental health and substance abuse social workers, $35,410. Median annual earnings of salaried mental health counselors are $34,380, with the majority earning between $26,780 and $45,610.

Self-employed counselors who have well-established practices, as well as counselors employed in group practices, usually have the highest earnings, as do some counselors working for private firms, such as insurance companies and private rehabilitation companies.

Sample Jobs

The following sample job advertisements will give you an idea of the qualifications needed, the responsibilities, and the salary levels that different job titles offer. When you are ready to look for employment, an Internet search should provide you with numerous available positions.

Forensic Psychology Postdoctoral Fellowship

The Law-Psychiatry Program of University Medical School, expects three positions for a one-year postdoctoral forensic psychology fellowship, administered in collaboration with the Forensic Division/State Department of Mental Health, Department of Correction, and State Hospital. The positions focus on work with adult forensic populations. The program offers: supervised forensic clinical evaluation and consultation experience at inpatient forensic units and court clinics; other minor rotations in a variety of forensic settings; seminars covering a broad range of topics within forensic psychology as well as review of landmark case law; and supervised research on issues in mental health law.

Requirements for applicants include a Ph.D./Psy.D. in psychology from an APA/CPA-accredited program with APA/CPA-accredited predoctoral clinical internship. Salary: Stipend $33,600 plus $2,000 support for educational/research expenses.

Mental Health Technician

To work under the supervision and direction of the program director, charge nurse, or staff nurse. Performs various duties assisting nursing and clinical staff in the treatment and care of patients in accordance with established policies and procedures.

Requirements include an associate degree in mental health with specified clinical practicum in a mental setting preferred. Persons with degrees in human services will be given consideration. Current CPR certification required. Salary: $9.45 to $14.20 per hour.

Forensic Psychologist

State prison is seeking a forensic psychologist to develop institutional policies and a treatment program for offenders, based on psychological theory and research within the prison system. Duties include undertaking research projects to evaluate the contribution of specific initiatives within the prison; evaluating research and statistical data; counseling offenders to manage depression, anger, anxiety, and other presenting problems; delivering special group or therapy programs such as sex offender programs and training/counseling of prison officers; and assessing "lifers" throughout. Additional self-employment/freelance work is possible.

Requirements include a Ph.D. in forensic psychology. Range of typical starting salaries: $30,000 to $46,000.

Inpatient Forensic Psychiatrist

Unique clinical and clinical/academic opportunities for inpatient civil and forensic psychiatrist(s) in a state-of-the-art, university-affiliated, public psychiatric hospital.

Positions feature: reasonable workload, forty-hour workweek, flexible schedule, minimal to no on-call duty, paid extra-service option, and treatment of challenging patients in the context of a multidisciplinary team. Positions also offer: weekly faculty-led case conferences, residency/fellowship didactics, and CME (all on-site). There is potential for: academic appointment at the university medical center, resident teaching in the long-term care program, involvement in a forensic fellowship known for training excellence, as well as research participation (schizophrenia, SPMI, psychiatric service delivery, psychopharmacology, forensics, psychophysiology).

Requirements include solid diagnostic and psychopharmaco-logic abilities. Experience in one or more of the following areas is strongly desired: SPMI, MICA/drug abuse, forensics, or geriatric psychiatry.

Benefits include competitive salary, retirement program, tax deferred savings plan, four weeks' paid vacation after one year, twelve paid holidays per year, excellent medical coverage, free dental/optical coverage, on-site day care, and employee assistance program.

Firsthand Accounts

Two professionals have shared their accounts. Read their stories to learn what working in this field is really like.

William Foote, Forensic Psychologist

William Foote began his work in this field in 1973 when he was employed by the New Mexico State Penitentiary as a psychological counselor. He received his B.A., his master's, and his doctorate, all in psychology, from the University of New Mexico. He has been self-employed in his own private practice for twenty-five years.

Getting Started

Dr. Foote became interested in forensic psychology while working as a counselor at the New Mexico State Penitentiary. He conducted a number of psychological evaluations and did some psychotherapy with inmates. He became intrigued by the relatively normal pres-entation of individuals who had committed very serious crimes. This work led to his research interests.

He conducted his doctoral research during an internship at a maximum security hospital in California. The research focused on people labeled as "psychopaths," who seem relatively normal but have no sense of connection with other people and often commit heinous crimes.

Subsequently, he began his private practice, which consists of conducting evaluations in both civil and criminal cases. He also qualified as a diplomate by the American Board of Forensic Psychology, which means that he is recognized as a specialist functioning at a high level of competence in the area of forensic psychology. Diplomate status is earned by experience and by passing a work sample review examination as well as a difficult oral examination.

What the Work Is Like

Dr. Foote explains that forensic psychology is a broad area, generally involving the use of information from a field of psychology in a legal setting. In his case, forensic psychology refers to the use of clinical psychology in legal matters.

On the criminal side, he conducts evaluations with individuals who have committed a range of crimes. Some of these, called "competency to stand trial" evaluations, are designed to determine whether the person has enough awareness of what is going on to participate in his or her criminal defense.

He also conducts "insanity" evaluations to determine whether the person was suffering from such a severe mental disease or disorder at the time he or she committed a crime that the law does not hold him or her criminally responsible. In addition, he conducts evaluations to determine the best course of treatment or incarceration for an individual at the time of sentencing.

He has worked on a number of death penalty cases, presenting information to the jury that would influence the severity of the penalty—that is, to deliver the death penalty or to choose a less severe alternative such as life in prison.

Sample Cases

Dr. Foote recalls a case in which a girl falsely accused her grandfather of sexually molesting her and where his expert testimony was critical in a not-guilty verdict for the accused.

In some cases, his input has helped bring about an appropriate outcome that would not have been possible otherwise. For example, a woman who was insane at the time she committed a dual murder was going to face a trial where she would have very likely been convicted and gone to jail. Based on Dr. Foote's discussions with the defense counsel, the prosecutor, and the judge, she was committed to the state hospital, where she completed treatment and eventually graduated from college.

Dr. Foote explains that forensic psychological evaluations are complex and take many hours to complete. He begins by reviewing records, which may include police reports, crime scene photos, laboratory results, and witness statements. He may also review the defendant's school, medical, and psychiatric records. Next he administers a battery of tests to the person, including personality tests and intelligence measures, and tests to ascertain whether the defendant is trying to appear more sick or well than he or she really is. He then talks with the person for two to twelve hours, which allows him to gather a history and learn about the person's problems and strengths. He usually puts all of this together in the form of a written report.

In civil suits, Dr. Foote does a great deal of work in employment discrimination cases, including sexual harassment and cases involving the Americans with Disabilities Act. He finds these cases interesting because they involve the interaction between an individual and his or her job. The evaluation process is similar to that used in criminal cases, although in civil cases the records may be different. Most civil cases involve depositions, which are sworn testimony taken by a court reporter. In discrimination cases, employment and Equal Employment Opportunity Commission records also may be important.

Upsides and Downsides

What Dr. Foote likes most about his job is the variety of people with whom he works. At one end of the spectrum, he works with people who are the least capable of functioning in society and must spend most of their lives in prison. At the other end are individuals to whom bad things have happened, such as automobile accidents. These people are often quite normal but are reacting to extreme circumstances in their lives with extreme emotional reactions. He appreciates being able to help these people receive proper treatment and to help a judge or jury to understand what has happened to them.

What he likes least is the tension and stress associated with testifying in court. He says, "In this situation there is at least one person in the room who wants to make you look foolish. Preparing sufficiently to withstand cross-examination and to present sometimes complex information to a judge and jury is often difficult. Keeping one's wits and focus during cross-examination is also sometimes hard."

Salaries

Dr. Foote reports that salaries for forensic work tend to be about 15 to 20 percent above what is charged by psychotherapists in the community. Most forensic psychologists charge by the hour, and those in private forensic practice generally have higher earnings.

Advice from a Professional

Dr. Foote explains that bridging the gap between legal standards and clinical results is at the core of the job. For this reason, forensic psychologists must have sufficient training in the law to understand legal terms, the legal system, and the language of legal codes and court decisions.

Another critical part of forensic psychology is translating information from this very specialized field into language that a judge or jury can understand. He says that this is hard to do at times because the concepts are relatively esoteric and the judges or juries to whom they must be communicated are relatively unsophisticated. In many ways it is like a teaching job in which educating a group of people is your primary task.

His advice for anyone wanting to be a forensic psychologist is to begin by obtaining solid training as a clinical psychologist. This means graduating with a bachelor's degree in psychology, followed by a master's and doctoral degree in clinical psychology.

Training in psychological testing and interviewing is critical. One option is to train as a clinical psychologist, followed by an internship or a postdoctoral fellowship at a penal or clinic setting. A number of graduate schools offer forensic psychology graduate programs, and several universities offer joint degree programs that lead to simultaneous Ph.D. and law degrees. Dr. Foote says, "If I had it to do over again, I would probably follow that course.

"The forensic psychologist, no matter who hires him or her, is in the court to provide unbiased information to the court," advises Dr. Foote. "There are pressures from those who hire you to come up with results that support their case. This is a pressure that most experts are aware of and for which they attempt to compensate. However, pressures arise from other sources in ways you might not anticipate. For example, sometimes when dealing with someone who has had bad things happen to him or her, you have to guard against becoming overly sympathetic or gullible.

"The other side of that coin is the temptation to become angry with individuals who have injured or killed helpless people or children. It is only by stepping back and attempting to maintain a neutral perspective that you are able to provide the judge or jury with information that is truly helpful, as opposed to voicing just another biased view."

He stresses that forensic psychologists are scientific experts who have to make sure that the quality of their work meets scientific standards. They accomplish this through the proper administration of tests, proper interview techniques, and systematic use of documentary sources such as school and medical records.

"Forensic psychology is a fascinating and challenging field. It requires the very best of the psychologist's work, both in conducting high-quality evaluations and consultations and in imparting accurate information to the judge and jury. The temperament required of a forensic psychologist is somewhat different than that of most psychologists who do psychotherapy. Forensic psychologists have to be able to think critically, to organize their thinking systematically, and to talk about what they know in terms that anyone can understand.

"It is work that sometimes involves big stakes. Large amounts of money, years in prison, or even a person's life depends upon how well the forensic psychologist does his or her work.

"It is also work that makes a difference. To make the legal system more fair and better informed makes ours a better society."

Jan Bailey, Psychiatric Technician

Jan Bailey is a licensed psychiatric technician in the forensic unit of Metropolitan State Hospital in Norwalk, California. She received her training in a three-year college program and has been working in the field for more than twenty-five years.

Getting Started

Jan says that she has always been interested in what makes people tick and enjoys helping others.

While she was working as a nurse's aide at a private medical hospital, the director of nurses asked for a volunteer to work on the understaffed psychiatric unit. No one wanted to go, but Jan volunteered for the job. She recalls, "Everyone else breathed a sigh of relief that they didn't have to go, and I got my first introduction to working with psychiatric patients. I loved it from the get-go and decided to enroll in a psychiatric tech program to get my state license."

The program she chose was a three-year college program that included prerequisites for the California Psychiatric Technician program. She passed the state board examination and was issued her license by the California Board of Vocational Nurses and Psychiatric Technicians.

To maintain her license, Jan must complete thirty continuing education units every two years. She is also required to take upgrade classes yearly to retain employment at Metropolitan State Hospital and must pass special forensic training classes to work inside the forensic compound within the hospital grounds.

In her first years at the hospital, Jan enjoyed her work in the chronic schizophrenic units. But as time went on, she began to take interest in patients in the forensic unit who needed understanding professionals to help them.

She says, "I had heard that the forensic units were the wave of the future and that, although these units were more dangerous when there was an altercation, the patients didn't seem to 'go off' as often as did the schizophrenics.

"I began to see forensics as a way to branch out my services as a psych tech. I began volunteering to float to the forensic units whenever they found themselves short of help. Finally I made my decision to go over to the other side of the fence."

What the Work Is Like

Jan works with prisoner patients who are transferred to Metropolitan State Hospital from other hospitals while waiting for their court appearances. Many of the patients are labeled as schizophrenic and are there waiting to become competent to stand trial. Although some really are schizophrenic, most are suspected of malingering or lying so they can serve their sentences in the relative comfort of the forensics ward, rather than await trial in a jail. The longest they can be held before trial is three years, and most hope to spend those years at the hospital and then have their charges dropped and be returned to society.

The hospital isn't necessarily expected to cure these patients but rather to make them understand the charges against them and the workings of the judicial system as it applies to their individual cases.

Jan describes the forensics compound within the state hospital as a highly secure area with guard gates on all sides, a high fence topped with razor wire around the perimeter, and video cameras mounted on all sides. With all the hospital police surveillance and the sophisticated alarm system within the compound, she finds it a safe place to work, which allows her time to concentrate on helping the patients rather than worrying about her own safety.

She says that inside the compound the prisoners and "dangerous" criminals become just as normal and human as anyone else. They need someone to help them bridge the gap between institutionalization and the outside world. Sometimes they committed their crimes when they were young or when they were under the influence of drugs. Sometimes they were in the throes of full-blown schizophrenia and simply needed to be put on medication. It's amazing how normal these people are when they are not committing crimes. They are someone's father, brother, sister, son, daughter, or friend.

Jan says, "My job is like being a mother to forty-eight men, most of whom are in their mid-thirties and early forties, with a range of from eighteen years of age to the early seventies. Actually, the job feels like being at home with my 'second' family, only I have forty-eight kids, some of whom are older than I am. But all of them treat me respectfully and as someone they know and trust."

She works the 3:00 to 11:00 P.M. shift. The pace is busy up until about 8:00 when dinner is over, and then it slows down for an hour of charting. When she arrives, Jan gets her assignment from the shift leader. Since jobs are rotated, her assignment usually differs every day.

She typically spends the first hour making sure the men shower and have clean clothing, after which they have a patio break to get some fresh air. Then it's time for dinner and day-hall leisure skills, such as watching the evening news.

Next the patients receive their medications, followed by the distribution of any special items or foods the patients have bought with their own money, which is handled through their trust office account. Each patient receives $12.50 per month, plus whatever their families have sent them to put in their accounts.

After specials and evening snacks, the patients settle down to watch movies rented through a contract with a local video store. The state provides some money on an account, and the staff goes to the video store and selects a current movie. When that money runs out, staff will usually bring in movies from home for the patients to watch.

Jan works forty hours per week and, given her length of service at the hospital, she is able to have Fridays and Saturdays off.

Upsides and Downsides

What Jan likes most about her work is knowing that she has worked hard to qualify for her position as guardian, mentor, director, and friend to people in trouble who seriously need someone to listen to them and offer educated help. The job is highly specialized and professional. It pays far above normal salary and offers great benefits and vacation packages.

She enjoys working the swing shift. Being off until 2:00 in the afternoon gives her time to take care of personal matters before leaving for work.

The aspect of the job that Jan likes least is the occasional danger of volatile and potentially violent patients. The state provides mandatory annual Management of Assaultive Behavior (MAB) classes to train the staff in how to work together to control assaultive patients through parry-and-evade tactics, rather than relying on strength alone. There are also classes intended to teach the staff to handle any possible cons that the patients might attempt.

Salaries and Benefits

Jan says that salaries in a forensic psychiatric unit are generally a bit higher than those in other settings. In addition, there are lots of opportunities for overtime. Employees receive eleven paid holidays per year. Vacation time varies but usually averages out to thirteen hours per month at the top of the scale.

Advice from a Professional

Jan suggests that if you can't find a psychiatric technician program, you should enroll in an R.N. program. Nurses do basically the same work as psychiatric technicians, with an added level of paperwork. But psychiatric technicians are more heavily involved with the psychiatric end of nursing, which may better suit your interest in forensics.

She offers this advice: "You can work as a certified nurse's aide while going through the program to familiarize yourself with the medical/psychological field and hospital settings. That way it won't seem so overwhelming to you when you set foot in the forensics department of nursing.

"If you enjoy helping people, are flexible in your thinking, work well under pressure and as a team member, this is the career for you."

A Final Thought

You have seen that forensic psychology and psychiatry offer possibilities in several areas. From social work to nursing to doctoral-level studies, you can find the foundation for a rewarding career in this area of forensic science.

7

EMERGING FORENSIC
SCIENCE FIELDS

THERE ARE SEVERAL additional areas in which forensic specialists may apply their skills. These branches of the forensic sciences have become more prominent in the last decade, in answer to advances in technology and a growing awareness of different types of crimes.

They offer an opportunity for computer analysts, accountants, economists, engineers, architects, and wildlife experts to pursue a career that combines their expertise with forensic training.

Forensic Computer and Cyber Investigations

It's difficult to imagine anyone not using a computer today. Most of us own a desktop or laptop or use one at a library or other facility, and nearly every business has incorporated the computer into its daily operations. Given this proliferation of computer use, it isn't surprising that people have found ways to use its technology for negative purposes. This has opened an entire field for computer forensic investigators who specialize in tracking computer crime and collecting evidence. Reasons a company might need a computer forensic investigator include:

- Theft of proprietary information
- Violations of company Internet use policy
- Tracking suspicious activity
- Improper use of company e-mail
- Collection and preservation of evidence for use in legal proceedings

Many large companies retain staff members to provide these services, but this field is also an opportunity for qualified individuals to work as freelancers.

The Internet has changed our lives in many ways, from how we pay our bills to how we apply for jobs and communicate with friends. Unfortunately, the Internet has also advanced the ability of criminals to target victims for a variety of illegal acts, whether they seek to steal financial data or promote pornography.

Given the pervasiveness of the Internet in our work and personal lives, it is not surprising that an entire field has emerged to deal with the problems of cyber crime. As an example of the areas in which forensic cyber specialists operate, consider the four-part mission of the FBI's cyber action teams:

- To stop those behind the computer intrusions and the spread of malicious code
- To identify and thwart online sexual predators who use the Internet to exploit children and to produce, possess, or share child pornography

- To counteract operations that target U.S. intellectual property, thereby endangering national security and competitiveness
- To dismantle national and transnational organized criminal enterprises engaging in Internet fraud

A recent example of the use of technology for forensic purposes is the case of Christopher Paul Neil, a pedophile who was caught by cyber sleuthing. Neil posted more than two hundred photos on the Internet of himself abusing young boys. In the photos, the boys' faces were visible while Neil's was hidden by manipulation of the digital images. German police were able to unscramble the images to identify the man's face, which led to a global manhunt and Neil's eventual capture.

In another case of child pornography, police were able to identify the furniture and wallpaper in a series of online photos and trace a pedophile to a specific hotel.

Training

To work as a forensic computer or cyber examiner, you will need the basic skills required of other computer specialists. A bachelor's degree in computer science or information systems is a prerequisite for some jobs; other positions may require only a computer-related associate's degree. Completing an internship is an excellent way to gain experience and is generally viewed favorably by potential employers. As in most of the positions we have covered, earning an advanced degree will improve your chances for advancement. A growing number of schools now offer degrees in computer forensics. These programs are generally found in departments of criminal justice or information science.

You will most likely start your career in an entry-level position in the computer specialization that you choose, such as support, programming, systems analysis, database administration, or software engineering. Regardless of the area, you will need strong problem-solving and analytical skills, as well as the ability to communicate effectively on paper, via e-mail, or in person, perhaps as an expert witness in a court of law.

As you gain more experience, you can advance to positions of greater responsibility. The more experience you acquire, the better suited you will be to a position in forensic computing.

Certification

The International Society of Forensic Computer Examiners (ISFCE) offers certification for qualified professionals. The designation Certified Computer Examiner (CCE) signifies that an examiner has met the high standards for this universally recognized certificate. A number of companies and government agencies require the CCE as a condition of employment.

Applicants for the CCE must meet minimum experience and training requirements, pass an online exam, successfully perform actual forensic examinations on three test media, and have no criminal record.

The certification process includes the following:

- Essential forensic computer examination procedures
- Rules of evidence for computer examinations
- Acquisition, marking, handling, and storage of evidence
- Chain of custody
- Basic networking theory
- Basic data recovery techniques

- Authenticating Microsoft Word documents and interpreting metadata
- Basic CDR recording processes
- Basic password recovery techniques
- Basic Internet issues

The initial CCE process consists of a proctored online multiple-choice examination and the forensic examination of a floppy disc, a CDR disc, and an image of a hard disk drive. After successful completion of the exam, applicants may begin the forensic examination of the test media.

Certified examiners are required to pass proficiency tests every two years and to fulfill experience or continuing education requirements. They must also adhere to the ISFCE code of ethical standards and professional responsibility.

For complete information on the certification process and the locations of authorized training centers, visit the ISFCE site at www.certified-computer-examiner.com.

Salaries

Salaries in computer-related professions vary depending on experience and responsibilities. Median annual earnings of computer and information scientists in research are $93,950, with the majority earning between $71,930 and $118,100. Median earnings of computer and information scientists employed in computer systems design and related services are $95,340.

Database administrators have median salaries of $64,670; most earn between $48,560 and $84,830. Those employed in computer systems design and related services average $72,510, and those in management of companies and enterprises, $67,680.

Median annual earnings of network systems and data communication analysts are $64,600. The majority earn between $49,510 and $82,630.

Forensic Accounting

Specialists in forensic accounting are able to combine their accounting and auditing expertise with the investigative skills needed to assist in legal matters. They are involved in litigation support, where they quantify the damages sustained by parties involved in legal disputes. In some cases, forensic accountants assist in resolving disputes before they go to court; in other cases, they may testify as expert witnesses.

Forensic accountants are also involved in investigation. In this capacity, the focus of their work is to determine whether criminal activities have occurred. These acts may include securities fraud, employee theft, insurance fraud, and identity theft, among others. They may also recommend actions to minimize future losses.

Forensic accountants also work on civil cases. For example, they may be hired to search for hidden assets in a divorce case or in the case of a contested will.

Training

There is no way around the fact that you will need extensive training to work as a forensic accountant. Most accountant and auditor positions require at least a bachelor's degree in accounting or a related field, and you can use this to gain experience while preparing to advance your career. To work as a forensic accountant, you will generally need a master's degree or extensive accounting experience. In addition, you can increase your opportunities by becoming a certified public accountant (CPA).

In recent years, most states have begun to require CPA candidates to complete 150 semester hours of college coursework—an additional thirty hours beyond the usual four-year bachelor's degree. In response to this trend, many schools have altered their curricula accordingly, with most programs offering master's degrees as part of the 150 hours. Be sure to carefully research accounting curricula and the requirements of any states in which you hope to become licensed.

All states use the four-part Uniform CPA Examination, which is prepared by the American Institute of Certified Public Accountants (AICPA). The two-day CPA examination is rigorous, and only about one-quarter of those who take it each year pass every part they attempt. Candidates are not required to pass all four parts at once, but most states require candidates to pass at least two parts for partial credit and to complete all four sections within a certain period. The CPA exam is now computerized and is offered quarterly at various testing centers throughout the United States. Most states also require applicants for a CPA certificate to have some accounting experience.

Accountants practicing in Canada may become chartered accountants (CA). To fulfill the rigorous requirements for this designation, you must complete a professional training program that is approved by an institute of chartered accountants and twenty-four to thirty months of on-the-job training with a CA in a recognized training office. The final requirement is to successfully pass the three-day uniform evaluation exam. You can then pursue an additional specialist designation in forensic accounting.

Sample Program

Following is a masters of accounting in the forensic accounting graduate program offered by Florida Atlantic University:

First Year
Fall: Accounting Fraud Examination Concepts
                Accounting for E-Commerce
Spring: Graduate Communications
                Concepts of Federal Income Tax
Summer: Accounting Fraud Examination Conduct
                    and Procedures

Second Year
Fall: Forensic Accounting and the Legal
                    Environment
                Advanced Accounting Information Systems
Spring: Litigation Services in Forensic Accounting
                Forensic Accounting, Fraud, and Taxation
Summer: Advanced Auditing Theory and Practice

Salaries

According to a salary survey conducted by the National Association of Colleges and Employers, bachelor's degree candidates in accounting received starting offers averaging $46,718 a year in 2006; master's degree candidates in accounting were offered $49,277 initially.

General accountants and internal auditors with up to one year of experience earn between $31,500 and $48,250 a year, depending on size the of the firm, location, level of education, and professional credentials. Those with one to three years of experience earn between $36,000 and $60,000. Senior accountants and auditors earn between $43,250 and $79,250 annually, and managers earn between $51,250 and $101,500. Salaries for directors of accounting and internal auditing begin at about $68,000 but may be as high as $200,000 based on professional experience and employment setting.

In the federal government, the starting annual salary for junior accountants and auditors is $28,862. Candidates with superior academic records might start at $35,752, while applicants with master's degrees or two years of professional experience begin at about $43,730. Accountants employed by the federal government in nonsupervisory, supervisory, and managerial positions averaged $78,665 a year in 2007; auditors averaged $83,322.

Forensic Economics

Professionals in this specialty of forensic science apply economic theories and methods to the issue of monetary damages as specified by case law and legislative codes. They are employed in business and government and are often asked to investigate claims involving individuals, employees, companies, and markets.

Forensic economists are hired to calculate damages in personal and commercial litigation and analyze claims to find evidence concerning damage liability. They are expected to employ generally accepted forensic economic methodologies and principles.

Training

Forensic economics is not a field for beginners; it is one that requires a great deal of education, preparation, and experience. Most forensic economists have a Ph.D. in economics; in fact, a master's or Ph.D. in economics is required for many private-sector economist jobs and for advancement to more responsible positions. Others who pursue careers in forensic economics are certified public accountants or have graduate degrees in business or finance.

Economics includes numerous specialties at the graduate level, such as advanced economic theory, econometrics, international economics, and labor economics. You should select a graduate school that is strong in the specialty in which you are interested. As an undergraduate economics major, you may choose from a variety of courses, ranging from microeconomics, macroeconomics, and econometrics to more philosophical courses, such as the history of economic thought.

You will need strong quantitative skills to work as an economist, so graduate courses in mathematics, statistics, econometrics, sampling theory and survey design, and computer science are extremely helpful. Some schools help graduate students find internships or part-time employment in government agencies, economic consulting or research firms, or financial institutions prior to graduation.

To gain an entry-level position with the federal government, you must have a bachelor's degree with a minimum of twenty-one semester hours of economics and three hours of statistics, accounting, or calculus. Whether you work in government, industry, a research organization, or a consulting firm, an undergraduate degree is usually sufficient for entry-level positions as research assistants, for administrative or management trainee positions, or for various sales jobs. You will most likely need a master's degree to qualify for more responsible research and administrative positions. In addition, many businesses, research and consulting firms, and government agencies look for applicants who have strong computer and quantitative skills and can perform complex research.

While in college, you should gain experience gathering and analyzing data, conducting interviews or surveys, and writing reports on your findings. This will prove invaluable later in obtaining a full-time position in economics because much of your work, especially in the beginning, may center on these duties. With experience, you will eventually be assigned your own research projects.

To be successful as an economist, you must be able to pay attention to details because much of your time will be spent on precise data analysis. You'll also need patience and persistence in order to spend long hours on independent study and problem solving. Good communication skills are also essential, particularly if you plan to work in forensic economics so that you can clearly present your findings in written reports and as an expert witness in court.

Salaries

Median annual wage and salary earnings of economists are $77,010. Most earn between $55,740 and $103,500, while the lowest 10 percent earn less than $42,280, and the highest 10 percent earn more than $136,550.

In the federal government, the starting salary for economists having bachelor's degrees is $35,752. Those with master's degrees could qualify for positions with an annual salary of $43,731. Those with Ph.D.s could begin at $52,912, and some with experience and an advanced degree could start at $63,417.

Forensic Engineering

Forensic engineering involves the investigation of structures, materials, or products that fail or that do not operate or function as intended, causing personal injury or other losses. A forensic engineer conducts an investigation to locate the causes of such failures, generally with the intent of improving performance or to assist in determining the facts of an accident.

Forensic engineers may work in a variety of areas. In manufacturing, they monitor products at early stages to correct failures and improve quality. For example, the failure of appliances or medical devices can cause serious damage and injury, so correcting any potential problems is critical. They may also work with insurance companies to determine liability in such cases.

Most of us probably associate forensic engineering with large-scale disasters. The 1907 collapse of the Quebec Bridge into the St. Lawrence River (and second collapse nine years later); the disintegration of the space shuttles *Challenger* and *Columbia* in 1986 and 2003, respectively; the 1996 crash of TWA Flight 800 in New York—these are just a few examples of engineering disasters that have required the expertise of forensic engineers. Perhaps the largest example of a forensic engineering case is the 2001 terrorist attacks that brought down the World Trade Center, an occurrence that still generates engineering questions years later.

Training

Forensic engineering is a specialized practice of the engineering sciences, not a separate discipline. Since few universities offer courses in forensic engineering, you must develop your own credentials. Most specialists perform their services part-time in addition to other work, such as college teaching.

You will need a bachelor's degree in engineering for almost any entry-level job. While most degrees are granted in electrical, electronic, mechanical, or civil engineering, you can train in one branch and work in related areas—for example, many aerospace engineers have training in mechanical engineering. This flexibility allows employers to meet staffing needs in new technologies and specialties in which engineers may be in short supply. It also allows engineers to shift to fields with better employment prospects or to those that more closely match their interests.

Some engineering schools and two-year colleges have agreements that will allow you to obtain your initial engineering education at the college and then be automatically admitted to the engineering school for your last two years of study. Some colleges and universities offer five-year master's degree programs, and some five-year or even six-year cooperative plans combine classroom study and practical work, which will allow you to gain valuable experience and to finance part of your education.

Graduate training is essential if you hope to secure an engineering faculty position and for many research and development programs, but it is not required for the majority of entry-level engineering jobs. Many engineers obtain graduate degrees in engineering or business administration to learn new technology and broaden their education; in fact, many high-level executives in government and industry began their careers as engineers.

To major in engineering, you will need a solid background in mathematics (algebra, geometry, trigonometry, and calculus) and science (biology, chemistry, and physics), with courses in English, social studies, and humanities. Bachelor's degree programs in engineering typically are designed to last four years, but you may find that it takes closer to five years to complete your studies.

All states and provinces require licensure for engineers who offer their services directly to the public. In the United States, licensure generally requires a degree from an engineering program accredited by the Accreditation Board for Engineering and Technology, four years of relevant work experience, and successful completion of a state examination. Engineers who are licensed are called *professional engineers* (PE). In Canada, engineers must meet the licensing requirements of their province or territory to gain the professional engineer designation of P.Eng. Many jurisdictions also have mandatory continuing education requirements for relicensure; check with your state or province for current policies.

Salaries

Engineers earn some of the highest average starting salaries among those holding bachelor's degrees. Following are starting salary offers for engineers in selected specialties, according to a 2007 survey by the National Association of Colleges and Employers:

Aerospace/aeronautical	$53,408
Architectural	$48,664
Bioengineering and biomedical	$51,356
Chemical	$59,361
Civil	$48,509
Computer	$56,201
Electrical/electronics and communications	$55,292
Environmental/environmental health	$47,960
Industrial/manufacturing	$55,067
Mechanical	$54,128
Nuclear	$56,587

Forensic Architecture

Along with forensic engineers, forensic architects investigate building collapses and related cases of structural defects or flaws. When called in on a case, a forensic architect will start at the beginning, evaluating the construction documents that defined the building process. This includes blueprints of the structure and specifications ordering the particular materials to be used in construction. The architect can study the entire construction process, considering such factors as the quality of materials, whether building codes were met, and whether subcontractors performed their work properly.

In many cases, the forensic architect is called upon to present findings in detailed written reports and to testify in courts of law.

Training

As with the other specialties in this chapter, you will need extensive training to work as a forensic architect. In addition to your training in architecture, you will have to master the investigative skills necessary to work on a forensics team.

To become a successful architect, you must be able to communicate your ideas visually to clients. Artistic and drawing ability is helpful in this area but not essential. More important are a visual orientation and the ability to conceptualize and understand spatial relationships. You will need good communication skills, creativity, and the ability to work independently or as part of a team. Computer literacy is also required for writing specifications, for two- and three-dimensional drafting, and for financial management.

In most areas, your professional degree in architecture must be from one of the schools that have degree programs accredited by the National Architectural Accrediting Board or the Canadian Architectural Certification Board. Three types of professional degrees in architecture are available. The majority of all architectural degrees are from five-year bachelor of architecture programs, intended for students entering university-level studies from high school or with no previous architectural training. In addition, a number of schools offer a two-year master of architecture program for students with a preprofessional undergraduate degree in architecture or a related area, or a three- or four-year master of architecture program for students with a degree in another discipline.

The degree you choose will depend on your preference and educational background, so you should carefully consider the available options before committing to a program. Your studies will typically include courses in architectural history and theory, building design, structures, technology, construction methods, professional practice, math, physical sciences, and liberal arts. Central to most architectural programs is the design studio, where you will practice the skills and concepts learned in the classroom.

Many schools of architecture also offer postprofessional degrees for those who already have a bachelor's or master's degree in architecture or other areas. Although graduate education beyond the professional degree is not required for practicing architects, it may be for research, teaching, and certain specialties.

You must be licensed to work as an architect in all states and provinces. Between graduating from architecture school and becoming licensed, you may work under the supervision of a licensed architect who takes legal responsibility for all your work. The licensing requirements include a professional degree in architecture, a period of practical training or internship, and a passing score on all divisions of the Architect Registration Examination (ARE).

Most localities will require you to complete a training period (usually three years) before you may take the ARE, which is offered at various testing centers throughout the United States and Canada. Most new graduates complete their training period by working as interns at architectural firms. If you complete an internship in an architectural firm while still in school, you may count some of that time toward the required three-year training period. You will be eligible to take the ARE after completing your on-the-job training period. The examination tests your knowledge, skills, and ability to provide the various services required in the design and construction of buildings. The test is broken down into nine divisions consisting of either multiple-choice or graphical questions. Once you pass the ARE and meet all standards established by your state or provincial board, you will become licensed to practice in that state or province.

Most states and provinces require some form of continuing education to maintain a license, and many others are expected to adopt mandatory continuing education. Requirements vary by jurisdiction but usually involve the completion of a certain number of credits annually or biennially through workshops, formal university classes, conferences, self-study courses, or other sources.

Salaries

Median annual earnings of salaried architects are $64,150. The majority earn between $49,780 and $83,450, while the lowest 10 percent earned less than $39,420, and the highest 10 percent earned more than $104,970. Those just starting their internships can expect to earn considerably less.

Wildlife Forensics

Wildlife forensics may be the newest field of forensic science to emerge. Several factors have led to the need for this profession, including poaching violations, the development of state and federal hunting regulations, the Endangered Species Act of 1973, and the

United Nations Convention on International Trade in Endangered Species.

Like any crime lab, wildlife forensic labs strive to identify evidence and link a suspect, victim, and crime scene through physical evidence. The major difference between criminal science and wildlife forensics is that the victim (and occasionally the suspect) is an animal.

Wildlife forensics is complicated by the fact that the evidence more commonly includes animal parts and products rather than whole animals. This makes identification difficult, since the characteristics that define an animal species are rarely present in those parts or products. To accomplish their work, wildlife forensic scientists must often develop new species-defining characteristics, through research with carefully documented known specimens, before they can examine evidence in a case and testify in court.

In addition, wildlife forensic scientists work with many different species and must be able to identify evidence from virtually any species in the world if it has been illegally treated.

The U.S. Fish and Wildlife Service reports that the following items of evidence have been examined by its National Forensics Laboratory:

- Blood samples
- Tissue samples
- Bones
- Teeth
- Claws
- Talons
- Tusks

- Hides
- Feathers
- Stomach contents
- Whole carcasses
- Weapons
- Asian medicinals (such as rhino horn pills or tiger bone juice)
- Leather goods

Training and Salaries

The training you will need to work in wildlife forensics is similar to what you would need in a corresponding position in a forensic science lab. Opportunities in this area exist for professionals in just about every area of criminalistics—pathologists, ballistics experts, accident investigators, technicians, computer analysts, and most of the other careers covered in the preceding chapters.

Similarly, the salaries you can expect to earn working in wildlife forensics will generally correspond to the salaries of professionals in any forensics lab.

If you enjoy working with animals and the environment, you might find a career in wildlife forensics very satisfying.

Sample Jobs

The following sample job advertisements will give you an idea of the qualifications needed, the responsibilities, and the salary levels that different job titles offer. When you are ready to look for employment, an Internet search should provide you with numerous available positions.

Senior Forensics Computer Examiner

Rapidly growing consulting firm seeks senior computer forensics specialist. Duties include supervising forensic technicians in imaging and restoring data; planning, budgeting, and managing forensic investigations; conducting detailed computer forensic analysis; testifying as an expert witness, if necessary; providing detailed reports; writing affidavits; and attending depositions.

Requirements include strong hands-on experience with computer hardware: laptops, desktops (including Macs), servers, networks, PDAs, and cell phones; 3-plus years of computer forensics experience in an investigative capacity; full understanding of chain of custody, federal search and seizure guidelines, and data collection; experience working in a legal setting—litigation, affidavit preparation, communicating with attorneys; excellent oral and written communication skills; ability to explain technical issues to clients, attorneys, juries, and laypeople. Salary: $80,000 to $130,000.

Forensic Engineer

Investigate and diagnose construction failures. Help to resolve construction-related disputes. Serve as a technical resource for nontechnical clients such as insurance adjusters and attorneys. Primary skills include observation, analysis, documentation, and communication. Salary: $45,000 to $75,000.

Forensic Accountant/Business Consultant

Leading litigation consulting firm seeks a forensic accountant/business consultant with good working knowledge of GAAP/GAAS and prior audit experience to work directly with one of the firm's partners on complex litigation cases, business valuation, and fraud investigation. The forensic accountant/business consultant will have involvement in professional associations and testifying experience, or the desire to testify. Salary: $100,000 to $122,000.

A Final Thought

This chapter shows you that there are opportunities in forensic sciences for nearly every level of professional. Introducing forensics to your studies in computers, accounting, economics, engineering, architecture, or wildlife can add a new dimension to a traditional career.

Professional Associations

Law

American Bar Association
321 N. Clark St.
Chicago, IL 60610
www.abanet.org

Evidence

American Academy of Forensic Sciences
410 N. 21st St.
Colorado Springs, CO 80904
www.aafs.org

American Academy of Psychiatry and the Law
One Regency Dr.
P.O. Box 30
Bloomfield, CT 06002
www.aapl.org

American Board of Criminalistics
www.criminalistics.com

American Board of Forensic Document Examiners, Inc.
7887 San Felipe, Ste. 122
Houston, TX 77063
www.abfde.org

American Board of Forensic Entomology
http://research.missouri.edu/entomology

American Board of Forensic Toxicology
410 N. 21st St.
Colorado Springs, CO 80904
www.abft.org

American Society of Crime Laboratory Directors, Inc.
139K Technology Dr.
Garner, NC 27529
www.ascld.org

American Society of Questioned Document Examiners
www.asqde.org

Association for Crime Scene Reconstruction
www.acsr.com

Canadian Society of Forensic Science
P.O. Box 37040
3332 McCarthy Rd.
Ottawa, ON K1V 0W0
www.csfs.ca

Forensic Entomology
www.forensic-entomology.com

The International Association of Forensic Toxicologists
www.tiaft.org

International Association for Identification
2535 Pilot Knob Rd., Ste. 117
Mendota Heights, MN 55120-1120
www.theiai.org

International Society for Forensic Genetics
www.isfg.org

Society of Forensic Toxicologists
One MacDonald Center
One N. MacDonald St., Ste. 15
Mesa, AZ 85201
www.soft-tox.org

Accident and Fire Investigation/Reconstruction

Aircraft Rescue and Fire Fighting Working Group
P.O. Box 1539
Grapevine, TX 77051
www.arffwg.org

Canadian Association of Fire Investigators
One Crimson Ridge Rd.
Barrie, ON L4N 8P2
www.cafi.ca

Federal Highway Administration
www.fhwa.dot.gov

Fire Department Safety Officers Association
P.O. Box 149
Ashland, MA 01721-1049
www.fdsoa.org

Insurance Institute for Highway Safety
www.iihs.org

International Association of Arson Investigators
2151 Priest Bridge Dr., Ste. 25
Crofton, MD 21114
www.firearson.com

International Association of Fire Fighters
www.iaff.org

International Society of Fire Service Instructors
www.isfsi

National Association of Professional Accident Reconstruction
Specialists, Inc.
www.napars.org

National Fire Academy
16825 S. Seton Ave.
Emmitsburg, MD 21727
www.nfaonline.dhs.gov

National Fire Protection Association
www.nfpa.org

National Highway Traffic Safety Administration
www.nhtsa.dot.gov

National Safety Council
www.nsc.org

National Transportation Safety Board
www.ntsb.gov

Northwestern University Center for Public Safety
http://server.traffic.northwestern.edu

Transport Canada
www.tc.gc.ca

University of Michigan Transportation Research Institute
www.umtri.umich.edu

U.S. Department of Transportation
www.dot.gov

Medicine

American Association of Colleges of Nursing
1 Dupont Circle NW, Ste. 530
Washington, DC 20036
www.aacn.nche.edu

American Association of Colleges of Osteopathic Medicine
5550 Friendship Blvd., Ste. 310
Chevy Chase, MD 20815-7231
www.aacom.org

American Board of Independent Medical Examiners
www.abime.org

American Board of Medical Specialties
www.abms.org

American Board of Medicolegal Death Investigators
1402 S. Grand Blvd.
St. Louis, MO 63104-1028
www.slu.edu/organizations/abmdi

American Board of Pathology
P.O. Box 25915
Tampa, FL 33622-5915
www.abpath.org

American Dental Assistants Association
35 E. Wacker Dr., Ste. 1730
Chicago, IL 60601-2211
www.dentalassistant.org

American Dental Hygienists' Association
444 N. Michigan Ave., Ste. 3400
Chicago, IL 60611
www.adha.org

American Medical Association
Dept. of Communications and Public Relations
515 N. State St.
Chicago, IL 60610
www.ama-assn.org

American Nurses Association
8515 Georgia Ave., Ste. 400
Silver Spring, MD 20910-3492
www.nursingworld.org

American Osteopathic Association
142 E. Ontario St.
Chicago, IL 60611
www.osteopathic.org

American Society for Clinical Pathology
1225 New York Ave. NW, Ste. 250
Washington, DC 20005
www.ascp.org

American Society of Forensic Odontology
www.newsasfo.com

American Society for Investigative Pathology
9650 Rockville Pike
Bethesda, MD 20814
www.asip.org

Association of American Medical Colleges
2450 N St. NW
Washington, DC 20037-1131
www.aamc.org

Association of Faculties of Medicine of Canada
265 Carling Ave., Ste. 800
Ottawa, ON K1S 2E1
www.afmc.ca

Canadian Association of Pathologists
774 Echo Dr.
Ottawa, ON K1S 5N8
www.cap.medical.org

Canadian Association of Schools of Nursing
99 Fifth Ave., Ste. 15
Ottawa, ON K1S 5K4
www.casn.ca

Canadian Dental Assistants' Association
1750 Courtwood Crescent, Ste. 205
Ottawa, ON K2C 2B5
www.cdaa.ca

Canadian Dental Hygienists' Association
www.cdha.ca

Canadian Medical Association
1867 Alta Vista Dr.
Ottawa, ON K1G 3Y6
www.cma.ca

Canadian Nurses Association
50 Driveway
Ottawa ON K2P 1E2
www.cna-nurses.ca

Canadian Osteopathic Association
P.O. Box 24081
London, ON N6H 5C4
www.osteopathic.ca

International Association of Forensic Nurses
www.iafn.org

Medical Council of Canada
www.mcc.ca

National Association of Medical Examiners
www.thename.org

United States and Canadian Academy of Pathology
3643 Walton Way Ext.
Augusta, GA 30909
www.uscap.org

Anthropology and Archaeology

American Anthropological Association
2200 Wilson Blvd., Ste. 600
Arlington, VA 22201
www.aaanet.org

American Board of Forensic Anthropology
www.csuchico.edu/anth/ABFA

Archaeological Institute of America
656 Beacon St., 6th Fl.
Boston, MA 02215-2006
www.archaeological.org

Association for Political and Legal Anthropology
www.aaanet.org/apla

Canadian Anthropology Society
www.casca.anthropologica.ca

Canadian Archaeological Association
www.canadianarchaeology.org

National Association for the Practice of Anthropology
www.practicinganthropology.org

National Association of Student Anthropologists
www.aaanet.org/nasa

Society for American Archaeology
900 Second St. NE, #12
Washington, DC 20002-3560
www.saa.org

Society for Applied Anthropology
www.sfaa.net

Psychology and Psychiatry

Academy of Behavioral Profiling
336 Lincoln St.
P.O. Box 6406
Sitka, AK 99835
www.profiling.org

American Academy of Psychiatry and the Law
www.aapl.org

American Association of Psychotherapists, Inc.
www.angelfire.com/realm2/hypnosis

American Board of Forensic Psychology
www.abfp.com

American Psychiatric Association
www.psych.org

American Psychological Association
www.apa.org

Canadian Academy of Psychiatry and Law
www.caplnet.org

Canadian Psychiatric Association
www.cpa-apc.org

Canadian Psychological Association
www.cpa.ca.org

Social Work and Mental Health Counseling

American Counseling Association
www.counseling.org

Association of Social Work Boards
www.aswb.org

Canadian Association of Social Workers
www.casw-acts.ca

Canadian Counseling Association
www.ccacc.ca

Commission on Rehabilitation Counselor Certification
www.crccertification.com

Council on Social Work Education
1725 Duke St., Ste. 500
Alexandria, VA 22314-3457
www.cswe.org

National Association of Social Workers
750 First St. NE, Ste. 700
Washington, DC 20002-4241
www.socialworkers.org

National Board for Certified Counselors, Inc.
3 Terrace Way
Greensboro, NC 27403
www.nbcc.org

Computer Investigation

International High Technology Crime Investigation Association
www.htcia.org

Accounting

Alliance for Excellence in Investigative and Forensic Accounting
277 Wellington St. West
Toronto, ON M5V 3H2
www.cica.ca

National Association of Forensic Accountants
6451 N. Federal Hwy., Ste. 121
Fort Lauderdale, FL 33308
www.nafanet.com

Economics

National Association of Forensic Economics
www.nafe.net

Engineering

National Association of Forensic Engineers
174 Brady Ave.
Hawthorne, NY 10532
www.nafe.org

Further Reading

Journals

Forensic Science Communications
www.fbi.gov/hq/lab/fsc/current/descript.htm

International Journal of Forensic Computer Science
www.ijofcs.org

Journal of the American Society of Questioned Document Examiners
www.asqde.org/journal_e_journal.htm

Journal of Forensic Sciences
www.blackwellpublishing.com/journal.asp?ref=0022198&site=1

Books

Forensic Science

Candilis, Philip J. et al. *Forensic Ethics and the Expert Witness*. New York: Springer, 2007.

James, Stuart H., and Jon J. Nordby, eds. *Forensic Science: An Introduction to Scientific and Investigative Techniques*, 2nd ed. Boca Raton, Fla.: CRC, 2005.

Kubic, Thomas, and Nicholas Petraco. *Forensic Science Laboratory Manual and Workbook*, 2nd ed. Boca Raton, Fla.: CRC, 2005.

Forensic Evidence

Buckles, Thomas. *Crime Scene Investigation, Criminalistics, and the Law*. Clifton Park, N.Y.: CENGAGE Delmar Learning, 2006.

Gennard, Dorothy. *Forensic Entomology*. New York: Wiley, 2007.

Kiely, Terrence F. *Forensic Evidence: Science and the Criminal Law*, 2nd ed. Boca Raton, Fla.: CRC, 2005.

Koppenhaver, Katherine M. *Forensic Document Examination: Principles and Practice*. Totawa, N.J.: Humana Press, 2007.

Maltoni, Davide. *Handbook of Fingerprint Recognition*. New York: Springer, 2003.

Newton, Michael. *The Encyclopedia of Crime Scene Investigation*. New York: Checkmark Books, 2007.

Robinson, Edward M. *Crime Scene Photography*. Burlington, Mass.: Academic Press, 2007.

Accident and Fire Investigation

De Haan, John D. *Kirk's Fire Investigation*, 6th ed. Upper Saddle
River, N.J.: Prentice Hall, 2006.

Icove, David J., and John D. De Haan. *Forensic Fire Scene
Reconstruction*. Upper Saddle River, N.J.: Prentice Hall, 2003.

Rivers, R.W. *Evidence in Traffic Crash Investigation and
Reconstruction: Identification, Interpretation and Analysis of
Evidence, and the Traffic Crash Investigation and Reconstruction
Process*. Springfield, Ill.: Charles Thomas, 2006.

Wheat, Arnold. *Accident Investigation Training Manual*. Clifton
Park, N.Y.: CENGAGE Delmar Learning, 2004.

Forensic Medicine

Adelman, Howard C. *Forensic Medicine (Inside Forensic Science)*.
New York: Chelsea House Publications, 2006.

Bowers, Michael C. *Forensic Dental Evidence: An Investigator's
Handbook*. Burlington, Mass.: Academic Press, 2004.

Dolinak, David, et al. *Forensic Pathology: Principles and Practice*.
Burlington, Mass.: Academic Press, 2005.

Hanzlick, Randy. *Death Investigation: Systems and Procedures*. Boca
Raton, Fla.: CRC, 2006.

Lynch, Virginia A. *Forensic Nursing*. St. Louis, Mo.: Mosby, 2005.

Stevens, Serita. *Forensic Nurse: The New Role of the Nurse in Law
Enforcement*. New York: St. Martin's Press, 2006.

Forensic Anthropology

Burns, Karen R. *Forensic Anthropology Training Manual*, 2nd ed.
Upper Saddle River, N.J.: Prentice Hall, 2006.

Byers, Steven N. *Introduction to Forensic Anthropology*, 3rd ed. Boston: Allyn and Bacon, 2007.

Nafte, Myriam. *Flesh and Bone: An Introduction to Forensic Anthropology*, 2nd ed. Durham, N.C.: Carolina Academic Press, 2007.

Forensic Psychology and Psychiatry

Howitt, Dennis. *Introduction to Forensic and Criminal Psychology*, 2nd ed. Boston: Longman, 2006.

Rogers, Richard, and Daniel W. Shuman. *Fundamentals of Forensic Practice: Mental Health and Criminal Law*. New York: Springer, 2005.

Rosner, Richard. *Principles and Practice of Forensic Psychiatry*, 2nd ed. London, England: Hodder Arnold, 2003.

Super, Donald E., and Charles Super. *Opportunities in Psychology Careers*, 3rd ed. Chicago: McGraw-Hill, 2008.

Walker, Lenore E. A., and David Shapiro. *Introduction to Forensic Psychology: Clinical and Social Psychological Perspectives*. New York: Springer, 2003.

Computer Forensics

Brown, Christopher L.T. *Computer Evidence: Collection and Preservation*. Boston: Charles River Media, 2005.

Jones, Keith J., et al. *Real Digital Forensics: Computer Security and Incident Response*. Upper Saddle River, N.J.: Addison-Wesley, 2005.

Accounting

Crumbley, D. Larry, et al. *Forensic and Investigative Accounting*, 3rd ed. Chicago: CCH, Inc., 2007.

Hopwood, William, et al. *Forensic Accounting*. Chicago: McGraw-Hill, 2007.

Engineering

Bosela, Paul A., and Norbert J. Delatte, eds. *Forensic Engineering*. Reston, Va.: American Society of Civil Engineers, 2006.

Architecture

Paegelow, Dale M. *Forensic Architecture: An Introduction*. Patterson, N.Y.: Cromlech Architect, 2001.

Wildlife Forensics

Cooper, John E., and Margaret E. Cooper. *Introduction to Veterinary and Comparative Forensic Medicine*. Oxford, England: Blackwell Publishing, 2007.

Murphy, Brian L., and Robert D. Morrison. *Introduction to Environmental Forensics*, 2nd ed. Burlington, Mass.: Academic Press, 2007.

ABOUT THE AUTHOR

BLYTHE CAMENSON IS a full-time writer with more than four dozen books to her credit, most on the subjects of various careers. She is the coauthor of *Your Novel Proposal: From Creation to Contract* (Writer's Digest Books) and director of Fiction Writer's Connection, a membership organization for new writers, which you can find at www.fictionwriters.com.